The Trick Horse Companion

Advance Praise

Allen is the best of the many trick trainers I have seen.

"Key among several innovative concepts of horse training I fervently believe in, for the benefit of the horse that both Allen and I share is:

Horses should not be started under saddle until mature (at 4 or 5 years of age). I know as a veterinarian that countless horses are prematurely crippled by excessive work before maturity. There are many things that can be taught from the ground before saddle training including trick training!

Allen is dedicated to the training of the newborn foal, a method I conceived of more than half a century ago and which is now successfully being used all around the world, in all disciplines and in all breeds."

– Dr. Robert M. Miller, DVM

Dr. Miller is, One of the best known horsemen and authors of our time is also an equine behaviorist and veterinarian, best recognized for his system of training newborn foals known as imprint training. http://www.robertmmiller.com/

Discover how good your relationships with and how happy your horses can be.

"It simply never occurred to me that a horse could reason, much like a dog can reason. Nor that the horse could develop a verbal vocabulary, like our movie superstar Benji.

I don't believe I have ever heard a trainer or clinician use the word reasoning in reference to a horse, nor encourage the use of verbal cues until I discovered Allen Pogue and his Imagine A Horse methods. Now I know: horses can have fun! They can grow to understand words. Even sentences! And they are fully capable of reasoning. All of which strengthens relationship, intelligence, and willingness.

Thank you, Allen, for continuing my amazing journey of discovery. My horses owe you and so so I."

– Joe Camp

Best-selling author of The Soul of a Horse* and film writer, producer, and director, author, passionate speaker and the man behind the canine superstar Benji,. http://thesoulofahorse.com/

I applaud the way Allen and Sue keep exploring the limits of what is possible in the horse-human relationship.

Allen Pogue and Suzanne De Laurentis caught my attention several years ago in the unique ways they combine the spirit of natural horsemanship with the best of traditional trick horse training. The result is an equine that willingly performs complex maneuvers at liberty with no signs of worry or uncertainty.

Best,

– Rick Lamb

Author of "Horse Smarts for the Busy Rider" and host of "The Horse Show" on RFD TV, www.thehorseshow.com also www.RickLamb.com

Sue and Allen are truly remarkable.
"Sue and Allen's understanding of animal behavior—equine in particular—is nothing like I have ever observed previously. It is deductive and complex and indicates such a deep understanding of equine behavior both generally (i.e., at the level of species patterns) and specifically (i.e., at the level of individual differences). Using this deductive knowledge in a way to engage horses in behaviors ("tricks") is remarkable to observe. Their understanding comes from many sources: extremely acute perception, intelligence, empathy and deep compassion for the animals they are working with. They have tapped into a communication channel (a "lingua franca" in its truest sense) that few will ever experience and I think it is brilliant. I can tell you that I have been working with animal scientists/academicians for decades and have never observed this previously... i.e., the translation of deep understanding into a hands-on practicum of interaction between human and another species."
– Joanna E. Lambert, PhD
Professor, The University of Texas at San Antonio
Fellow, American Academy for the Advancement of Science

"Trick training" can be an important part of any horse training program.
As a professor of animal science at Texas A&M University, I have been inviting Allen Pogue back to demonstrate his methods for training horses and to lead a discussion on the history of horse training with my classes every year for over a decade. All too often, horses are trained to the level needed for their primary use solely, and then are basically ignored as long as they perform at the expected level. Most additional or advanced training we might do with a horse falls into the "trick training" category. But such training represents a lot more than merely teaching a horse to do a simple trick. Advanced training increases the trust and communication between both the horse and rider. It can take both to a new level not otherwise possible. Allen Pogue is very well read and has mastered both the theory and implementation of advanced horse training.

– Dr. Ted Friend
Professor and Texas AgriLife Research Fellow - Department of Animal ScienceTexas A & M University

Highly Recommend!
"I have worked with Sue and Allen for many years and have filmed segments for my Speaking of Horses TV Show with them, too. They are very professional trainers. I highly recommend their work!."
– Wayne Williams
"Speaking of Horses" TV and Radio - www.speakingofhorses.com

The Trick Horse Companion
Your Complete Guide to Enlightened Trick Training

Allen Pogue
Suzanne De Laurentis

P O P Network, Inc.

The Trick Horse Companion

Your Complete Guide to Enlightened Trick Training

ISBN-13: 978-1497592148
ISBN-10: 1497592143

By Allen Pogue and Suzanne De Laurentis
© Imagine A Horse, 2014

Contributing Editor: Bobbie Jo Lieberman Weber

Contact the authors at: http://www.imagineahorse.com

Book Design by: www.martimcginnis.com

Contributing Photographers
Kate Austin, k8ace@yahoo.com
Marianne Martin, Reallifeportraits.com
Paula DaSilva, http://www.pauladasilva.com/
Penny Stone, http://wholehorsemanship.blogspot.com/
Jim Halfpenny, Back 40 Studios http://www.jameshalfpennymusic.com/
and *Texas Highways Magazine*

To my "Editor in Chief", Mother and Best Friend, Betty De Laurentis
You gave me the best beginning of life ever....instilling in me love of the West and of all animals and nature. You and Dad were the greatest of inspirations!
Your complete interest in my life plus thousands of hours of editing our work has meant more than words can say.
I love you all the way around the barn and back, Mommy Hen!
Your Little Chickie
Sue

From Sue
I rarely take enough time to thank Allen for all he has brought to my life and to our ranch. We met because I had a special mare, TF Eclaire, who gave us Navegador, our main exhibition horse and ambassador for our work.
The first time I saw Allen and Hasan, I fell in love with both of them. Hasan was a horse like no other, and his patience and talents were great. He was the first of many fine horses that we share. He was La Primera. We will surely spend our eternity in a paradise that includes Hasan and his herd. Thank you for believing in Allen, as I have.

Dedication

We dedicate our work to God in gracious thanks for his wonderful gift to mankind—the horse. Our horses are our "patient soldiers," beloved individuals who time and again interact willingly and obediently so you may learn. We hope you share these lessons with friends, both human and equine, for the rest of your life.

We are grateful for our life in this grand country, the United States of America, where we are free to pursue the expression of our dreams.
We are blessed indeed to also have each of you come into our lives.
Thank you for working with us and may God Bless You!

Sue and Allen

Table of Contents

PART I: Introduction to Enlightened Trick Training

PART II: A Toolbox of Tricks

Foreword

By Susana Gibson
Editor & Publisher, *trailBLAZER* magazine

In 2008, when I asked Sue De Laurentis and Allen Pogue to initiate a series of articles in *Trail Blazer* we would call "Take Tricks to the Trail," I had little idea of how far-reaching and groundbreaking this series would be.

Horse "tricks" have traditionally been thought of as "cute party pony tricks" that show a horse answering "yes" or "no" to a question or counting out his age with the tap of a hoof. More sophisticated tricks can look impressive, but we often had no idea how the horses were trained, or what gimmicks were used to produce the end result. The sad truth is that horses often suffered from some of the methods used in trick training. Sue and Allen's Enlightened Trick Horse Training is, to my knowledge, the first trick-training method that honors the horse's intelligence and individuality.

Throughout my 36 years of publishing *Trail Blazer*, I have always known that a smarter horse would make a safer horse, and a safer horse would bring trail riders more pleasure. Sue and Allen have brought this ideal into being in a way that is accessible and achievable by all riders.

"Taking Tricks to the Trail" became an exciting addition to *Trail Blazer,* with nearly 50 articles helping readers develop a better relationship with their horses. Trail riding is one of the most sacred of equine careers. A trail horse not only takes you to magnificent places, but more importantly, he brings you home safely.

This book is the first comprehensive how-to manual on the subject of equine trick training. Some of the moves are basic and easy to teach, laying the groundwork for more advanced moves. While you may not teach your horse "every trick in the book," you will have a broader perspective and understanding of equine behavior and insights into humane methods of educating our equine companions.

Enjoy the journey!!

The Trick Horse Companion

Preface

Allen's earliest life memory was being set down by his Grandmother in the feed bunk next to a draft horse. The image of that horse, whose head was a big as his small body is still vivid today. Later as a youngster, he and friends watched Saturday morning cowboy shows and then went out and tried to emulate the tricks and stunts of his favorite western heroes.

Sue's earliest memories included having her mom and dad set her on the back of a gigantic draft horse mare, Blondie. In just a couple of years, she was roping and branding dolls as substitutes to real calves. As a competent four year old rider, she followed her dad around the ranch on her own horse helping to check and doctor cattle.

Allen says "Starting at the age of thirty, I spent ten years trying to figure out what I wanted to do with horses, another ten years passed as I crafted a method of communicating with horses in a language that we both understood and more importantly, enjoyed. Half a lifetime is a mighty long time, yet not nearly enough time, to perfect the fine art of communication with horses. Living life in such a way that my horses are my life, has enabled me to really learn from them. My Arabian stallion, Hasan was a horse like no other and his generosity allowed me to achieve actual results that I had only imagined were possible. He was my first student of Enlightened Trick Horse Training and the cornerstone of Imagine A Horse methods".

"At age fifty, Sue entered my life bringing her experience and love of horses and a wealth of marketing skills. At the urging of a dear friend, P. J. Oliver and Sue, we began to introduce Imagine A Horse to an international audience through articles, DVDs, public appearances and now, the Trick Horse Companion".

We hope through sharing our life's work we may make it easier for you to truly engage with your horse in a fulfilling manner, and enjoy error free learning. That means we have already made all the mistakes so you won't have to!

Because your horses are truly individuals, we can't tell you exactly what will work with them. We can however, share what has worked with our horses and the student horses we have known.

It is an honor and a privilege to have you join us through our *Trick Horse Companion*.

Acknowledgements

Special thanks to those listed for allowing us to include your horses:

Lady C, Tennessee Walking Horse/Spotted Saddle Horse
Friends of Sound Horses,
http://www.fosh.info/
Mystic River, Tennessee Walking Horse/Spotted Saddle Horse
Sheryl Crow
Look's Champagne Illusion, Tennessee Walking Horse
Bobbie Jo Lieberman-Weber
Shotgun's Lady Athena, Tennessee Walking Horse
Bobbie Jo Lieberman-Weber
Yellow Blanket, American Quarter Horse
Schiller Ranch LLC
Holly, American Quarter Horse
Heather Hughes
Charisma, Morgan/Friesian
Patty Grimm
Dash, National Show Horse
Kate Austin
Miko, Miniature Horse
Tammy Peterson and Sallie Ingle
Rafiq, Arabian
Tammy Peterson and Sallie Ingle
Sophie, Miniature Horse
Carol Curran
Charra, Miniature Horse
Judith Mc Culley
Pusher Rocks, Tennessee Walking Horse/Spotted Saddle Horse
Carobeth Bennett
Sebastian, Mustang
Kaitlin Sheehan
Cash Benefit, Miniature Donkey
Sisu Morris, Stockmarket Donkeys
Salute, American Paint Horse
Mariann Jones
Cal, Morgan
Kristi Reavis

Isabelle, Lusitano/Arabian
Mary Stewart
Shallana, Arabian
Donna Moore

Horses from Imagine a Horse

Elk Hasarn, Arabian
Navegador, Lusitano/Arabian
Dos Sangre, Lusitano/Arabian, Grandson of Hasan
Senor Unico, SP
Deano, Missouri Fox Trotting Horse
Boullet, Missouri Fox Trotting Horse
Marzouk, Half Arabian
Amharanni Ibn Hasan, Arabian
R Monet, Arabian
Sharrifah, Arabian
Sombra de Estrella, Lusitano/Arabian
Estrela de Tabajara, Lusitano/Arabian,
Visten, Tennessee Walking Horse
Alyah, Arabian, Alyah bint Hasan
Hasana, Arabian, Hasana, bint Hasan
Beso Elegante, Andalusian

Note-
"ibn" in Arabian horses' names indicates a male is a son of a particular stallion.

"bint" indicates the daughter of a particular stallion.

How to Use this Book

The first time I saw Allen's horses perform, it was inspiring and beautiful. Hasan, a beautiful Arabian stallion and his daughter, Alyah performing in complete confidence, in unison and compliance. While I dreamed of such a relationship with my own horses, I thought "How would this ever be possible for me?" What was most amazing about Allen's horses was how involved and interested they were in "**playing**" with him.

Although I had been with horses since two years of age and considered myself to be well educated in conventional horsemanship, Allen's philosophies and strategies in training were absolutely new and revolutionary to me.

Soon, with Allen's patient coaching I began to digest the concepts of Imagine A Horse. I carefully mimicked his style with faith of achieving similar results. In time, Allen's words became my own, his patience and expectations were easier to duplicate and the responsiveness and interest of my own horses increased.

We hope that you are amazed and inspired by "The Trick Horse Companion". You may initially be overwhelmed. Although we have structured the content for those who approach learning and training in a linear fashion, there is absolutely no mandatory sequence to applying the philosophies and instructions.

As you peruse the book, you may wonder as I did, if the more complex and intricate moves will be achievable. Once you begin the journey of Enlightened Trick Horse Training, the rapidity of your progress and success will surprise you. This will be due to a combination of your enthusiasm and of your horse "learning to learn" in a brand new and revolutionary way.

With our student horses, we begin simultaneously with the Smile and Pedestal Training. These teach elementary concepts and cues and increase the horse's confidence and convince him that you can be trained.

If you have been struggling with a trick or move and wish to add clarity and finish to it, it is acceptable to go directly to that segment and proceed with our method. Your horses will begin to benefit immediately from whatever content seems most interesting and pertinent to your situation.

All categories of Tricks or moves fit together seamlessly and build upon each other to result in a highly- educated and responsive horse. A horse who is truly a companion, an individual who will enrich your life whether in sport, play, or competition. A "*Trick Horse Companion*" of your own.

Sue and Allen

Until one has loved an animal, a part of one's soul remains unawakened.

– Anatole France

PART I:
Introduction to Enlightened Trick Training

The Sit Down is a combination of Tricks of Trust and Tricks of Agility.

A Brief History of Trick Horses

Everybody loves a trick horse. In the days of early Westerns featuring stars such as Roy Rogers and Gene Autry, trick horses were commonly referred to as "high school" horses, borrowing the term from classical dressage or haute école.. Trigger, Champion and other equine heroes were household names and widely admired for their beauty and talent. Western stars and their accomplished equine partners almost always had a circus connection. According to one account,

"At the end of the 1920s, 'outdoor' under-canvas shows began hiring well known motion picture western stars as feature attractions. During the golden age of the Hollywood western films in the 1920s and 1930s, the five big stars were Tom Mix, Buck Jones, Ken Maynard, Hoot Gibson and Tim McCoy. All were featured with circuses. A number of them worked with circuses before their film careers started. Some started their own circus or wild-west show." — James Searles, author of "Cowboys and their Horses"

Despite this rich heritage, the usual contemporary trick-horse image evoked is one of a horse acting out silly skits, pawing to count and answering posed questions with a "yes" or "no" motion of his head. It is the modern norm that trick horses are used to display humans' ideas of comedy, usually through a few very basic tricks, a simple behavior chain or an obligatory curtsy or partial bow.

During the Middle Ages, itinerant troupes of players known as gypsies trained their horses to curvet and caracole as they performed alongside dancing bears and other animal entertainers. Later, Renaissance riders recognized and endeavored to embellish the beauty of the horse's natural gaits. Early circus acts reflected the art of high school horses performing the conventional gaits of the haute école but also unusual movements such as cantering backwards and on three legs along with various dance and march steps. These theatric representations were spectacles and included the conventional as well as the absurd.

The strict confines of modern dressage is only a reflection of the grand spectacles presented in carousels and tournament parades that would feature a score of horses performing the High School airs simultaneously. When classical baroque dressage and historic circus training, with enchantment of the audience the only expectation, are combined, the result is circensic dressage.

In the late 18th century, the modern circus emerged in England, which took its name from the Latin word for ring. By limiting the size of the schooling and performance area, a trainer could hold a horse's attention, resulting in a high degree of compliance. The size also lent itself to liberty acts, in which the audience could be seated close to the horses. This stage style presentation of horse handling contributed readily to the infant movie industry after the turn of the 20th Century. Westerns were popular. Horses were still an integral element of the American culture, and the perennial cowboy hero was always saved by his equine co-star.

Most recently, international equine "spectaculars" such as Cavalia, Oddyseo and Apassionata have done much to express the true nobility and magnificence of the horse and bring them to a wide audience.

Why We Do Enlightened Trick Training (ETT)

We use trick training as a means of increasing the intelligence, adaptability, predictability and desire of today's companion horse to interact with us. "Companion" signifies the horse is elevated in his relationship with us and is a pleasure to spend time with—and he is a safer horse. A companion horse may be a performance horse of any discipline or sport, a saddle or trail horse or a rescue horse.

One of the purposes we hold dear in our quest to modernize trick horse training is to put off saddle training of a horse until he reaches physical maturity. Our modern equine society demands a quick return on in-

vestment so much emphasis is on riding two-year-old horses. We hope to influence the training of young horses and foals by offering an alternative educational tool for an additional two years, when mounted work may be safely begun. The young years of a horse should be seen as an investment in itself, not a waste of time because he is not yet under saddle and producing revenue in futurities.

When the emphasis shifts from primarily

Pedestal Training can have many variations.

The Trick Horse Companion

Above and below:
Retrieving is a Trick of Engagement of Enlightened Trick Horse Training.

mounted sports to the higher education and physical longevity of the horse, one of our primary goals will be realized.

The idea that horses should be turned out during their most formative years to "learn how to be horses" seems absurd to us, as they are born knowing how to be horses. What would serve them better would be a world in which we help them to become productive and valued citizens in the world of humans.

Trick training encourages communication and desire for interaction from the horse. This in turn promotes willing obedience as he learns to engage and respond on a higher level. With engagement comes a new level of responsibility for you. You will no longer have a horse that will be happy when left alone in the pasture or caught up occasionally as your schedule allows. Your horse will come to the gate calling to you as you pass by, each time more insistent with his eagerness to play. When a horse has truly become your companion, he will plead for interaction for only a while before he gives up. Your new responsibility will be to be his companion in every sense of the word.

Every day our horses do things that make

The Bow is a Trick of Trust.

us laugh, yet we do not use tricks as the basis for comedy skits. We aspire to showcase their intelligence, beauty and nobility and not make them appear foolish. We endeavor to uplift the stature of the horse in our modern world and pay back in part the debt owed him by mankind.

Trick training helps strengthen our relationship with horses and gives them a type of behavioral language to reach out and interact with us. When a horse "smiles" or offers other learned (or spontaneous) behaviors, he is asking for interaction. Enlightened Trick Training includes teaching concepts and acceptable responses to cues, which help a horse understand how to engage with us in pantomime or by mimicry—copying or mirroring

our behavior. This is why trick horses smile, salute, pick up objects or step up on pedestals on their own, as a means of getting our attention. We actually encourage this type of interaction because we want the horse to know we will listen when he tries to communicate. Only a slave is told what to do by an uncaring master.

In many disciplines and styles of training, quick, rote responses are valued while personal opinions or preferences on the part of the horse are discounted and discouraged. In Enlightened Trick Training, we encourage equine self-expression because it promotes confidence and willingness to engage. This does not mean obedience is optional, but suggests a horse may be more willingly obedient when his ideas are of value to us.

Practical applications of Enlightened Trick Training are demonstrated in everyday situations such as trailer loading, veterinary treatment, working with the farrier and hoof trimmer, trail riding and occasionally during performance disciplines.

Enlightened Trick Training helps humans become better teachers. When a horse is under saddle, he can be manipulated physically

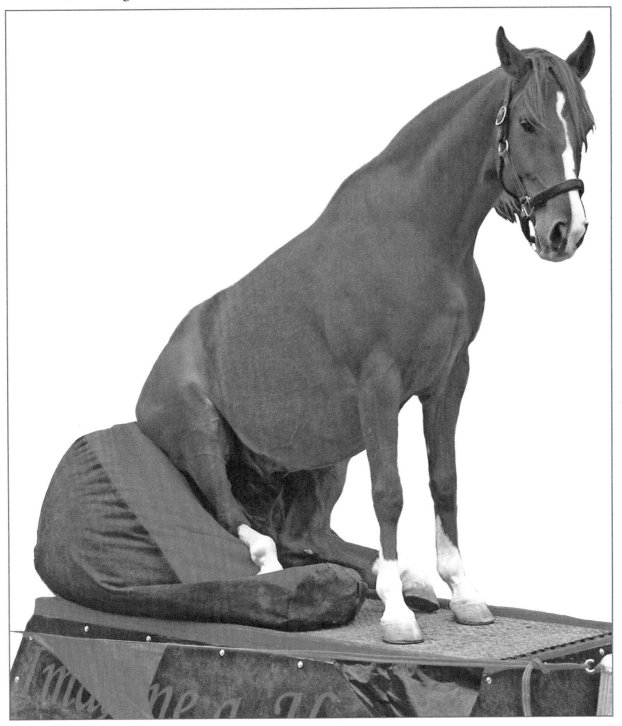

Navegador performing at the Cowboy Symposium in Ruidoso, New Mexico, in 2008.

with legs, bit, crop or other aids. In trick training, a horse must be coached and encouraged to learn, and ultimately he must want to engage. No amount of force or negative reinforcement training will result in a horse that will happily retrieve a Frisbee, herd a big ball or wave a flag!

Not all horsemen and women desire or possess the ability to interact with a horse on such a reciprocal, intellectual level, and some horses don't have the desire for a high level of interaction. When the desire of human and horse coincide, however, the relationship between them appears telepathic and magical.

Horses are a precocial species, meaning young foals are ready and able to learn soon after birth. We use an abbreviated form of Imprinting followed by age-appropriate challenges to help them accept humans as a normal part of their world. On our ranch, they grow up thinking all horses do tricks such as sitting on beanbags, retrieving caps and hopping up on pedestals. Our young horses are proven performers even as adolescents.

Dr. Robert Miller, one of the best known horsemen and respected equine authors of our time, says the results of our Enhanced Foal Training are so remarkable that until he actually saw what we were doing he would not have thought it possible. He has used snippets of our methods in his lectures worldwide for many years.

Joe Camp, creator of the Benji movies and bestselling author of "The Soul of a Horse," says Imagine A Horse training methods have made him much more aware of the mental capabilities of his horses, that horses can and do "reason."

Many folks do not have the luxury or inclination to raise their own horses. Trick Horse candidates can be weanlings or mature hors-

es retired from other careers and even rescue horses. They are never too old to learn!

We raise our own horses and have successfully trained many breeds of all ages. Candidates should be at least tolerant and social. Most moves or tricks require a horse be sound in body; however, many tricks are suitable for horses in rehabilitation.

Folks often ask us what is the best starting point for Enlightened Trick Training. It can begin at any age and integrates well with saddle training. There are six main categories of Trick Training linked together in a progressive sequence, making no individual trick mutually exclusive. You may decide on a particular starting point to serve your horse's needs or you may want to follow our progression; either way is perfectly acceptable.

The training instructions contained in this manual are researched and have been applied to hundreds of horses, yet are not intended as absolutes. Throughout the process, we advise that you be ready, willing and able to practice what is called Rapid Intelligent Failure or RIF. Simply put, if something isn't working, be quick to recognize it and change the approach.

The Spanish Walk is a Trick of Gait.

Dos Sangre and Navegador retrieving as a team at liberty.

Classical Training is an art and science. We've included reading resources to help in understanding classical training principles, which are not diluted to meet the needs of a generalized marketplace. If we had to choose only one book to start with it would be Henry Blake's "Thinking with Horses." It is a classic that uses understandable and workable terms to explain many training principles and explains how to utilize the horse's inherent nature to enhance training.

"It's Not Just Tricks"

Any specialized move a horse learns, such as a spin, slide, crossing a bridge, retrieving a Frisbee or taking a bow, is a type of trick. Enlightened Trick Training is not an end point but rather an educational journey and process of creating a high school horse, trail horse or dependable, adaptable companion horse.

Our philosophy is inspired by Alois Podhajsky, former director of the famed Spanish Riding School In Vienna. His motto was *"The goal in all training is to make the horse more beautiful."* The horse naturally is a noble being and his beauty is enhanced by individual expression, inspiration, cooperation and willing obedience. Enlightened Trick Training encourages a horse to "learn how to learn," promotes improvisation and gener-

ous latitude by the horse, which magnifies his beauty and showcases his intelligence.

We utilize plenty of props, including pedestals to mount, large balls to herd, small balls to retrieve, beanbags to sit upon, Frisbees to retrieve and cleat boards for targeting. Horses make powerful associations between objects (props) and actions, and by adding positive reinforcement including food treats, you can expect to see rapid results. Horses love this education because it is easy for them to understand and it's fun—not like work, but more like play. Most animal behaviorists agree horses are among the smartest of all domesticated animals. We believe they are capable of much more than is ever asked of them. Enlightened Trick Training can maximize your horse's personality, intelligence and desire to interact in a way that makes sense to him.

Knowing a few fundamental tricks could actually save your horse's life or at least make medical treatment easier. According to the book about Ruffian, *Burning from the Start*, this famous race mare came to her untimely end because she was so hot and difficult to handle that successful treatment of her broken leg was impossible. What if Ruffian had been taught while still a foal to lie down and remain down quietly? Would it have taken away her desire to run and to win? We don't know the answer, but lying quietly would have allowed her to be treated; her life depended on it.

What Makes a Trick Horse Candidate?

All breeds and ages are trick horse candidates yet learning is easiest for personable, energetic horses. A horse with playful tendencies and a desire to interact usually makes a great trick horse. Horses that seem dull or uninterested may not be the first choice; however, some actually perk up when introduced to it. It's easy to understand, and easy for them to be successful. Horses with a sense of humor make great candidates as do the Houdinis of the horse world—those that open gates, pick up objects to use as toys or ask to be fed by fetching feed pans.

As with any other discipline, preparation to teach your horse tricks requires him to have good manners. Teach basic ground skills and work out areas of resistance before you begin.

The props, equipment and preparation required are well worth the effort. We use single and multi-tiered pedestals, specially designed whips designed to convey a cue and Horse-TUFF Balls to help develop a horse's herding instinct and sense of play. Leather tabs on flags and Frisbees make them easy to pick up.

As a bonus, trick training can reduce a horse's stress level, as sequences are easy to understand.

We use food treats as a motivational tool, although a few horses just can't tolerate treats and maintain their good manners. Our DVD "Using Treats as a Training Tool" gives lots of instruction and tips on using food rewards responsibly and effectively.

The culmination of the categories of tricks is a horse or horses working at liberty and linking behaviors together in what we call a **Behavior Chain**.

Building Blocks of Learning

The six categories comprising the process of Enlightened Trick Training, outlined in the highlighted box on the facing page, seamlessly combine to culminate in the complete education of an exhibition horse. The starting point may be influenced by your goals and personality of your horse. ETT isn't necessarily designed to be remedial yet combining all six categories results in better behavior and understanding. We suggest following the educational flow contained herein although any category can be a suitable beginning.

Remedial lessons for a flighty horse may include pedestal work to help him be grounded, literally and figuratively. When a horse is longed on a working length line and asked to mount the pedestal and stand quietly, **the trick** quickly **becomes the reward** rather than the work. Revolving pedestals and multi-tiered pedestals provide challenging

A three-trick Behavior Chain—a Hind Leg Walk, Retrieve and landing on the pedestal.

ENLIGHTENED HORSE TRAINING CURRICULUM:
THE SIX BASIC CATEGORIES

Pedestal Training

Pedestal training might be called the centerpiece of our work. But amazingly, horses have traditionally not been trained in this manner. Big cats, birds, reptiles, elephants and dogs (canine agility) are all trained using a pedestal or "mark." We believe horses can benefit even more than other species because they are a flight animal. The pedestal gives a horse a piece of real estate to call his own and feel safe, a home base where he can take a break and receive praise. Pedestal work develops physical dexterity and increases self-confidence, boldness and a sense of security.

Tricks of Trust

Tricks of Trust include the **Obeisance** or **Circus Bow**, the **Bow**, **Kneel** and **Lie Down**. These are moves in which a horse learns to lower his eye and his body in relation to the handler's, putting him in a position of mental and physical submission, and requires great trust in his handler. "Submission" indicates a horse is agreeable and willingly responds to our requests and acknowledges our position as leader in his herd (of two). An example of submission is when a horse lowers his head willingly to allow the handler to place a halter or bridle on his head.

Tricks of Engagement

In retrieving an object such as a Frisbee, flag or cap, a horse willingly chooses to engage in the activity. This includes herding and retrieving a big ball. A horse cannot be forced but rather **chooses** to do them and engage. Willing engagement is a giant step in creating a **can-do attitude** that develops into a **want-to-do work ethic.**

Tricks of Agility

These include the **Salute** (Jambette), **Crossing the Front Legs**, the **Rear**, **Hind Leg Walk**, the **Sit Up** and **Sit Down** and gymnastic moves on pedestals.

Tricks of Gait

Tricks of gait include amplifications of natural movement as simple as an extended trot, cakewalk, march and culminating in the **Spanish walk**, **piaffe**, **passage** and **terre a terre.** Even the airs above the ground (levade, courbette and mezair) can be included.

Liberty Training

Liberty training is one horse or a troupe performing without any attachment (such as a lead or bridle) to the trainer. Liberty training begins in a small square pen or corral as the horse learns to **walk with** the handler, **halt**, make **inside turn**s and **circles** and **go to pedestals** as directed.

Another variation of liberty training is horses executing patterns solo, in pairs or in sets of pairs. A further variation includes horses performing numerous moves or elements of an act in a routine as directed by the handler. Our liberty performances include numerous pedestals used to define the patterns and as a place for one or more horses to stay while others perform.

variations and learning opportunities both mental and physical.

A horse lacking respect or compliance can gain these virtues with Tricks of Trust, as they require him to develop a submissive attitude. The Obeisance, Jambette and the steps required to learn the Spanish Walk help increase strength and range of motion in a horse's front legs and shoulders. With the Sit Down (on the beanbag), the horse relaxes every muscle in his top line, contracts ventral muscles and also rotates his pelvis underneath his body. As with yoga for people, extreme poses yield extreme physical results! Herding the big ball is an activity that brings out a horse's herding instinct and sense of play. Teaching a horse to retrieve will help develop the handler's training acumen. Liberty training can increase confidence and reliability in both the horse and the handler.

A person no longer able to ride or a fearful person can become energized with Enlightened Trick Training as it can unveil a dimension of their horse's personality they may not have known even existed.

Note: We normally don't teach "party pony" tricks such as counting or saying yes or no because they are ends in themselves and in addition, the horse is not really counting but waiting for a cue to stop pawing. In Enlightened Trick Training, each initial step is a building block in creating additional behaviors. A move such as the Jambette forms the basis for the Spanish walk, which is a classical move.

Trick Horse Training is a great way to have fun with your horse and for both of you to learn some really cool yet classical moves. We dare you to imagine the possibilities!

Horsemanship Principles

As with all other aspects of our lives, good horsemanship is governed by timeless, universal principles. We have included some examples from which you may formulate your own:

Horsemanship Principles
From Mary Twelveponies, author of *"There Are No Problem Horses, Only Problem Riders"*:

1. Have control of the horse
2. Give him an explanation in his language
3. Teach one thing at a time in proper order
4. Reinforce learned behavior through consistent repetition
5. Avoid confrontation

Visten in a perfect Sit Down.

**Horsemanship Principles
for Trick Training
From Allen Pogue:**

1. Select a horse with natural potential for trick training

2. Acknowledge the smallest try as you shape the approximations the horse offers

3. Control each situation, as you anticipate and prevent evasions.

4. Condition your horse to the sight, sound and feel of a guider whip in a friendly manner

5. Associate specific vocal, proximity and physical cues with each lesson

6. Teach new lessons in the smallest, yet safest, area to minimize distractions

7. Walk the horse through new patterns or moves

8. Two or three successful repetitions per session is enough

9. Allow generous free movement walkabout time between repetitions

10. Use treats responsibly—small rewards or praise for tries and larger jackpots for a breakthrough

11. Stop a lesson after a breakthrough

12. Be quick to recognize when a horse offers a useful variation

13. Never criticize or complain about your horse, especially in his presence

Non-riders can trick train a horse. It is the understanding of concepts, timing and time devoted that will give a successful outcome.

Handling horses on the ground allows observation time and furthers physical coordination and manual dexterity required to ride with empathy for the horse.

Avoid generalized desensitization methods that startle the horse. It is better to *sensitize* him to understand and respond appropriately to requests.

Always Maintain Your Horse's Trust

Practice Error-Free Learning, meaning teach in such a way that horses can easily and quickly understand requests. Too many repetitions make a horse dull and impart an attitude of hopelessness. "Practice makes perfect" is a human concept and doesn't necessarily apply to horse training. We believe "Perfect practice makes perfect" or in other words, Error-Free Learning.

Set a horse up for success, using methods, equipment and props to help him understand and respond to your requests.

Acknowledge and respect the Physical, Mental, Emotional and Spiritual aspects of the horse.

- Soothe and support your horse in his efforts to learn and to please you

- Promote calmness

- Every move you make means something to a horse, make each move count. Learn to be quiet with your body and mind

- Horses are capable of learning words and simple phrases if they are carefully taught the meaning. Separate vocal cues so they are distinct and practice using your voice as a tool

- Freedom of movement between repetitions keeps a horse's mind fresh

- Give your horse a great name and reputation to live up to

- Horses are generally more capable than humans believe

A nice Behavior Chain by Navegador - he mounted the pedestal and executed a Jambette working at liberty.

- Allow the horse dwell time between requests, on the ground and when mounted

- Educate yourself in the artful use of whips

- Learn each horse's style of compliance and degree of resistance

- Never give up on your horse!

- "Routine" or school a move in the same place, same position, with exactly the same cues until it is confirmed. Then "generalize" the behavior in new locations.

- Develop predictable Behavior Chains by linking separate tricks together

- Never do anything that upsets or startles the horse.

Good Will and Presentation

We enjoy a steady stream of visitors at Red Horse Ranch, and Allen and I always make time to show off our horses. Everybody loves a trick horse, and having one will create many opportunities for you to share your horse's talents and to honor the equine species.

A trick horse is a wonderful ambassador and testament to the beauty, intelligence and selflessness of one of God's greatest gifts. Trick horses are unique and wonderful. They

A colorful ring and props showcased Lady C's performance at BreyerFest 2013.

bring smiles, melt hearts and spread light and hope to humans.

The last visit my Arabian gelding Monet made to a nursing home is a wonderful memory to me. He suffered from COPD and was often grouchy when he rode in the trailer as it affected his ability to breathe. The day of our visit, he was especially out of sorts and I worried about his behavior among the seniors. As I brushed him, the folks lined up for a close look at my special horse. I felt rather helpless to cheer Monet up and simply said to him as I rubbed his face, "Monet, you have to be great AND gentle today because these folks need you." I envisioned him as his usual charming self, and his attitude changed almost immediately.

I will forever treasure the memory of Monet standing in the driveway while seniors in wheelchairs, on walkers, canes and wobbly legs flooded around him, talking to him, stroking him and offering an endless supply of carrots.

That afternoon of pure joy was worth every second that Monet and I spent training.

Pay Attention to Detail

When presenting your trick horse at a show or performance, attention to details such as good grooming will show you take pride in your horse. Props and pedestals in good condition and cheerful in color show your respect for the audience. Remember to dress appropriately for the venue, and never wear a cheap hat!.

Be prepared to ad lib. When performing with our horses, we have had some very interesting experiences, some more humorous than others! Expect the unexpected and enjoy the ride.

Hasan and Allen perfomring as Ausin Wranglers' mascot.

A few years ago, Hasan was the mascot for the Austin Wranglers Arena Football. We did not realize the AstroTurf was slippery, and, with Allen mounted, when he reared to his pedestal it slipped out from under him.

A nice presentation is never too much trouble.

complete with smoke and a fireworks show. As the director was calling for the two to exit the helmet and gallop onto the playing field, the helmet started to deflate onto them and trap them inside. Hasan was stuck and the artificial stage smoke filling the tent-like helmet sure did not help. The audience was not aware of the technical difficulty and cheered madly awaiting their appearance. Allen stayed calm as the stagehands struggled to free Hasan of the tangle of plastic that pushed Allen to lie over on his side. The two finally made their escape out of the giant, collapsed helmet and Hasan continued brilliantly with his performance. His faith in Allen's leadership was totally confirmed.

Here are a few performance pointers:

- When you present your horse and things are not going as planned, be quick to realize it and move on to something else without making a fuss.

- Do not make excuses to the audience for your horse, just keep the show going.

- If your horse offers a surprise variation to your routine, go with it. Our horses have often ad-libbed an entire section of a performance and done an astoundingly good job without the audience ever knowing it.

- Relax and your horse will relax too.

- Always be positive about your horse even if you think he flubbed the routine. If he wasn't talented, you wouldn't have attempted the performance.

Steadfast guy that he was, he kept following the pedestal, which was persistent in slipping out from under him.

At another game, Allen and Hasan were to gallop out of a giant inflatable football helmet

Navegador and Dos Sangre performing at Texas A&M University open house.

- If your full attention is on your horse, you won't be nervous.

- If you have not done public speaking or demonstrations, get coaching from a pro. A brilliant horse won't totally make up for a human's shortcomings.

- Smile, Smile, Smile.

- Never let them see you sweat the details.

Allelomimetic Behavior

Horses love to mimic other horses. The proper phrase for this is *allelomimetic behavior*. If there is a particular behavior that one of your friends does with his or her horse, ask if you may tie your horse in close proximity to observe. It is common practice in training young saddle horses to put one in the round pen and move him around while mounted on another horse. In this way student horses see a rider above eye level, and see being ridden is no big deal. Tethering horses in saddle or trick training, where they can observe the training of other horses, is also a good practice.

Our own horses and student horses have learned lots of tricks while watching their peers perform. They often present tricks we haven't taught them and we know the only way they could have learned is by watching, through allelomimetic behavior.

Progress and the Nature of Horses

A good understanding of horse nature is helpful in Enlightened Trick Training. There will be times during trick training, as with any other discipline, that your horse simply will not be able to understand your requests. Be patient and creative in your approach and try again. If your horse doesn't understand how you are attempting to teach him a move, change your language or requests until he literally gets the picture. Don't reprimand him for not understanding your requests. If you lose your patience, you lose his good will.

There is a fine line between lack of understanding, evasion and refusal. If you are certain your horse understands your request, don't be afraid to push through a difficult period. A horse will usually resist the most just before he gives in and offers the most. When a horse doesn't understand requests, it is usually because the answer is not obvious to him. Check your body position, your physical cues, your whip position and especially your mood and intention.

Expectations

Expect your horse to perform to the best of his ability. Expect him to occasionally question you. Expect times when you will be disappointed with his performance...and love him anyway. Expect him to surprise you with his brilliance. Disappointment serves no purpose—do not indulge in it.

Imagine A Horse training techniques have stood the test of time and yielded success with many, many horses. If you do not get immediate results, do not quit or give up. Horses learn and assimilate new information at individual rates, just as humans do.

Time and Devotion

The benefits of Enlightened Trick Training demonstrated by our horses are a result of many hours and months of effort and daily devotion. Many horses, such as our hot-blooded types, thrive on companionship, so trick training is a daily routine for them; they demonstrate often how much they enjoy it. For most horses, 20-30 minutes a day or even two 15-minute sessions will be adequate to learn the basics and even progress at a decent rate.

Equestrian Tact

"Tact is the ability to use the right aid at the right time with the right strength and the right duration."
–Francois Ruffieu
reflectionsonriding.com

Ray Hunt said to
Buck Brannaman:
"You need to do less sooner; you're always doing too much, late."

We've had lots of horses learn literally every trick in the book with sporadic training and over a long period of time. This is the beauty of understanding each horse's individuality! When horses have learned how to learn, progress is surprisingly quick.

Response and Anticipation

Horses tend to react quickly yet respond slowly to our requests. Give him plenty of "dwell time" between repetitions. It is the silence between the notes that makes the music! Trick training helps a horse to slow his reactions as he responds to our requests.

Horses should anticipate pleasing us although anticipation should not over-ride giving the correct response as cued. Mixing up routines will help control anticipation.

Understand your horse's learning signals or signs of satisfaction as well as his expression of frustration. Common displays of understanding include licking and chewing, letting out a deep breath or sigh, nodding or

Lady C bows for her fans at BreyerFest 2013.

dropping the head, nudging you and a look or feeling of relaxation. Common displays of frustration include tail wringing, swinging or shaking the head, ears pinned back, a furrowed brow, stomping of the feet and "zoning out."

Correction and Manners

Horses seem to have a magnified sense of justice and seem to appreciate fairness, especially the hot-blooded types. Strive to be fair in the treatment of your companion.

Refrain from punishment as it is generally emotionally charged and beyond a horse's ability to comprehend. Inflicting pain is always counterproductive. We simply ignore the wrong responses by turning our atten-

tion elsewhere. If a correction is necessary be quick, firm and without emotion. An honest horse usually accepts correction without holding a grudge.

At some point in EVERY horse/human relationship there comes a time when the horse will say (through his actions) "I don't want to, and I don't have to, and I'm not going to, because you can't make me." When this happens, you may make the choice to find a way to make the horse comply with your requests or a way to make your horse want to comply with your requests. This is your choice and your choice only. We take Ray Hunt's old adage, "Make the right thing easy and the wrong thing hard," a step further and strive to make the right response not only easy but fun.

Handler's Attitude

The most destructive words in the horse handler's vocabulary include:

- can't
- won't
- doesn't
- hasn't

Don't fall into the trap of saying no for your horse!

Focal Messages + Intention = Intuitive Horsemanship

Focal messages are clear thought pictures or messages we send to our horse. Focal messages generally communicate our intent. If we clearly picture the action we want from the horse and combine it with focus and concentration, the horse will begin to respond readily. Focal messaging is natural for some folks and not so much for others. We know through experience our results of focal messaging increase as our knowledge of our horse increases. Our horse friends have related hundreds of stories to us about their results with focal messages and intuition. We don't exactly know how or why it works, but we know it does work.

Focal messaging and intuitive thoughts flow freely between humans and horses. We'll share some of our experiences with a few stories later in this book.

Concepts and Cues

Enlightened Trick Training utilizes a full range of communication methods and cues. As with any new activity involving hand-eye (and horse) coordination, you may feel awkward initially, but the delivery of cues and aids will become natural and coordinated with practice. Do horses understand concepts? You be the judge!

We view concepts as what horses learn as the natural consequence or result of our cues and his actions. Both concepts and cues help to establish a sort of working dialogue between horse and handler. Concepts can be explained as the understanding or expectation of the horse (conditioned response) to words such as "Good Boy, Cookie Time, Ready, Try Again, No, Be Careful and Let Me help". Horses can easily learn the concept that the pedestal is a place to rest and receive praise, to be taller than the other horses.

Horses respond best to a combination of cues. Relying on just one cue, such as voice, touch or gesture will achieve limited results. Your voice is the direct connection to your horse's mind, and touch is the connection to his body, when you add habituation to consistent cues, results are more predictable.

6 Types of Cues

Preparation Cue

A preparation cue prepares the horse to focus mentally and physically on the task ahead. This cue alerts the horse a request is coming momentarily and is a call to attention with a word such as "Ready?" or simply saying his name prior to a request.

Physical Cue

A physical cue is a consistent, light touch to a particular part of a horse's body to indicate how you would like the horse to move or respond to your request.

Proximity Cue

A proximity cue is the position of your body in relation to the horse's body to help him interpret your request.

Verbal Cue

Your voice can be a lifeline to your horse in many diverse situations. Verbal cues should be delivered in a concise and timely precision and also must stand out from other chatter. Some trainers don't advocate the use of verbal cues because the concept of utilizing the voice as an instrument is not easily mastered.

Release Cue

The horse should be trained to hold each pose or continue with each task until he is given a release cue.

Energetic Cue

Horses are sentient, energetic beings and respond to our intention and projected energy. The effective modulation of our energy is understood and acted upon perhaps more quickly and effectively than a combination of all other cues. The horse instinctively reads our mind, soul and physical presence, and he will respond to the level of enthusiasm and motivation projected toward him. An example would be when we stand facing the horse on a pedestal and ask for the Jambette or Salute. If we merely raise a hand, he may slightly lift a leg yet if we speak encouragingly and enthusiastically, he will respond with a higher leg lift, mirroring our enthusiasm. Imagine a traffic cop directing you through an intersection in an animated yet friendly way as he uses his whole being's energy to pantomime his request.

Practice your cues on a human friend to make certain they are understandable.

Focal Messages

A focal message is your intention expressed as a mental picture you send to your horse. Your focal message will automatically help your body give cues to the horse to support his efforts to understand your request.

Think in complete sentences to help your horse literally "get the picture."

Bridge Signal

A bridge signal links your horse's response to a forthcoming reward. It's difficult to give a food reward instantaneously so your words bridge the horse's response and hold his expectation. The bridge signal is like the "Click" in Clicker Training (which is a great instrument to teach new trainers timing).

Rewarding the Horse

Most horses can be trained with a variable reward system. When a trick or move becomes a conditioned response, food treats may be replaced with verbal praise or stroking. Some horses can be trick trained without using food rewards, but we see an extra spark of brilliance from horses when they anticipate a food reward.

The following may help you better understand and implement methods for rewarding your horse using food treats.

Scratches can be a great reward.

Treats can be used to lure a horse into many positions, including a stretch.

Show Me the Motivation! Using Treats as a Training Tool

"If it eats, it can be trained" is scientifically and practically sound advice for training virtually every species of animal except traditionally, the horse. Everyone knows dogs work for food! Every domesticated species of animal trained by humans is trained using food treats. It is an acceptable standard practice; just watch the handlers dispense tidbits during dog shows and even canine agility. As a society, we tend to feed those we love, including our pets and as a result, food treats for pets, including horses, is big business.

But giving food treats to horses is a controversial subject. Some horse handlers frown on hand feeding horses and some dispense treats as though there were no tomorrow. "Some swear by it" and some swear at it is so true. So what's the truth of the matter of feeding horses treats?

Horses love food treats and are highly motivated by them. They are rapid learners with fabulous memories, enabling them to distinguish in about five seconds if a food treat is a given right, a gift, reward or a bribe. A horse's good manners can go south with the snap of a carrot! It is easy for the well-intended use of food treats to go wrong, which is exactly why many trainers don't advocate their use. But food treats can produce great results in shaping behaviors and training specific moves.

If you currently use food treats, give some thought to why you use them. Do you think treats will make your horse love you more or behave better? Do you feed treats because you love your horse? Be honest, no one can hear your thoughts!

Motivational Training

Horses are generally trained using the release of stimulus (often referred to as pressure), which in most cases can be an adequate reward especially if the release means a few seconds of physical rest. Equines bred for a particular sport or job, such as cutting horses, often find intrinsic (from within) reward in their work. With other horses, praise such as stroking or a kind word is an appreciated and adequate reward. But in some individuals and in certain situations, release of stimulus can be further enhanced with a food treat. Circus horses performing at liberty (no lead

Prevent Mugging—It's Easy (No Cookie Monsters Here)

You can prevent "mugging" in most horses by applying a training method to feeding treats. For any training method to work, the handler must be committed to it and apply it consistently.

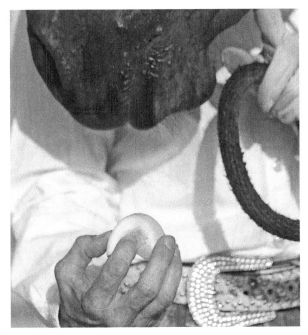

To retrain horses that mug for treats, use a slice of lemon.

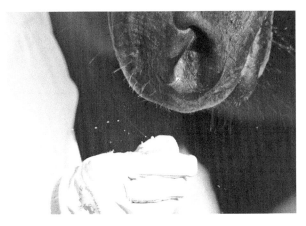

Hold it in your hand and give the horse a gentle spritz of juice if she comes into your space without a cue.

Plan your reward system before you start using treats and consider your own sequence, timing and verbal cues, including what name you will call a "treat." We use "cookie time" as our verbal signal a treat is coming. This is a "bridge signal" because it bridges the horse's behavior to the reward. If there is ever any doubt horses can learn to understand words, just try saying "cookie time" a few times followed quickly by producing a treat!

Sombra was happy to stay out of Sue's space!

ropes) are a good example of effectively using treats as a training tool. When teaching intricate maneuvers and long sequences or behavior chains, a food treat adds brilliance to a horse's performance and sparks the desire to learn.

Treats Basics

Commercial horse treats such as those made by *Start to Finish* (www.STFproducts.com) are economical to use, bite size and come in horse-appropriate flavors. Small bites are most effective in training. Larger treats require a lot of chewing and most horses will lose their focus of why the treat was given. Check the nutritional value of treats to be sure they will not affect your horse's specific health concerns.

If a horse gets food treats for reasons other than training, it may be best if they are fed from a bucket. "Using treats as a training tool" is an entirely separate matter and you will usually feed them by hand.

Tips for Treats:

- Some horses become aggressive and are therefore not candidates for training with treats

- Plan your training sessions and your reward system

- Wear gloves and always carry a whip

- Feed other peoples' horses with permission only

- Don't feed or carry treats when entering a group of horses

- Use a designated pouch for treats, not your pockets

Learning to stand quietly for mounting.

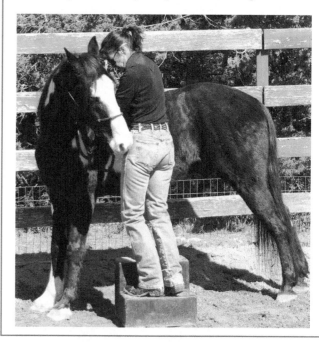

- Recognize your horse's efforts to learn and improve his performance

- Give a few seconds "dwell" or "thought" time between repetitions for mental absorption

- End each training session with your horse feeling successful

- Keep praise precise, methodical and timely

- Carrots should be cut into long slivers and apples into small chunks to prevent choking

- If you don't get the sequence and the timing right, treats won't work for you.

How We Do it at Imagine A Horse

We use treats as a training tool for trick training, agility training and for under-saddle work, such as opening a gate, learning to stand quietly for mounting and teaching a horse to come when called by name.

Here's the sequence we use:

1. Cue your horse for the move you want, such as "Smile."

2. When he responds correctly say "Good Boy" and stroke him. If his response was either an improvement over an earlier try or a very good response, add "Cookie Time" and give him a treat immediately. Three seconds is too long for your response.

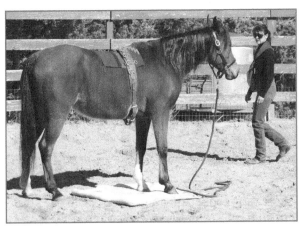

Sharrifah learning to ground tie.

Charra was not a good candidate for hand-held treats so she got her reward in a bucket.

Stop the Hold Up! (Or, Good Manners are for Horses, Too)

Some horses are overstimulated by food treats and clearly not candidates for their indiscriminate use. If your horse is conditioned to understand he will only receive a treat when he hears the magic words, he may never become pushy. If your horse becomes demanding, you may need to correct him. Stepping out of the horse's reach will help some horses understand not to invade your personal space. Correction does NOT mean punishment.

To correct a pushy horse, establish a bubble of personal space you expect your horse to stay out of. If it is two feet, then always make sure he stays out of that two-foot space unless you invite him into it.

We use a product called NipBuster (www.nipbuster.com) as an aid to control mugging and get our training back on target. It is a citrus-based spray and fits in the palm of the hand. When a horse enters your personal space without permission, quietly and

slice of lemon or lime works well too. A touch on the nose or a little spritz is usually enough of a deterrent that a horse won't be interested in invading your personal space, even to look for a treat. Never use any offensive tasting or smelling substance such as ammonia (or others) or hit or slap the horse! A horse will quickly slip back into any habit including mugging if you are not diligent. It's just horse

Nip Buster is a great tool to retrain a horse that mugs.

nature.

For more information, see our DVD *"Using Treats as a Training Tool"*

Treats can be a motivational tool to teach mounted skills such as opening a gate.

with no emotion spritz it in the vicinity of the horse's nose. NipBuster is harmless and since most horses don't like citrus, they happily retreat from your space with little reaction. A

Sharrifah respectfully accepted her treat after completing the entire gate sequence.

The Trick Horse Companion

Equipment and Props

Trick training is built around basic principles of shaping the horse's natural behaviors and responses. We use pedestals and props such as beanbags, big balls, small balls, toss-and-retrieve balls, Frisbees (modified), hobbles, surcingles, guider whips and more.

Toss and Retrieve Ball

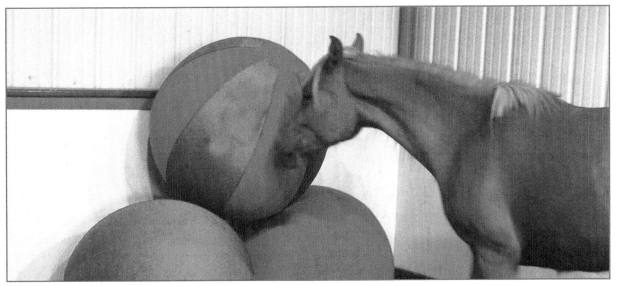

Horse Tuff Balls

Pedestals

Pedestals can be constructed in many dimensions. The standard sizes we start with are a 24" x 48" rectangular shape and a 36" x 36"square top. Heights can be from 12" to 15". Variations on construction styles are revolving-top pedestals and multi-tiered or stairstep pedestals and agility platforms.

If your horse is a draft breed, foal or mini, you may want to modify the size of the pedestal to accommodate his size. The approximate height is determined by measuring from the middle of the horse's knee to the ground. If that distance is 12 inches, use that number or a little less for the height that's right for your horse.

Pedestals are an integral component of Enlightened Trick Horse Training.

Pedestals can be customized to reflect your ranch colors or performance styles.

Agility Platforms can be made in different sizes or degrees of difficulty.

A smaller multi-tiered Agility Platform for advanced work.

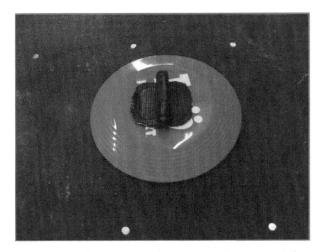

Frisbee with gripper tab sewn on for easy pick up.

Treat pouch clips easily to your belt or blue jeans.

Horse Friendly Whips

Cleat or Target Board

Surcingle and Belly Band with 3 rings

Climbing Wall

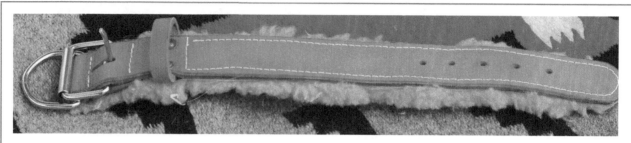

Sheepskin lined hobbles

Sheepskin lined hobbles

Horse Tuff Bean Bag

Liberty Pole

Allen and Elk Hasan executing a Courbette.

PART II:
A Toolbox of Tricks

The Smile

Smiles are contagious. When we walk into the barn and our horses start flashing us a big toothy smile, it makes us smile right back. Horses don't use a smile exactly the way we do but they do learn to offer a smile to try to engage with us. Teaching the Smile is a great exercise in developing your timing and ability to communicate with him.

The Smile is easy to teach most horses. It can be taught to a mouthy horse to give him an acceptable default behavior. The Smile on a horse puts a smile on most human faces and is a good beginning point to get to know your horse's personality and your aptitude as a trainer.

We have seen many horses use the Smile as a way of telling us they feel a trick has been performed satisfactorily or if he is obviously trying to communicate. The horse is actually teaching the human to give him a treat.

Equipment
Tidbit-sized cookies!

Goal
Convince the horse that when he talks, we will listen to him.

Benefits
Gives your horse an acceptable behavior he can use to communicate with you.

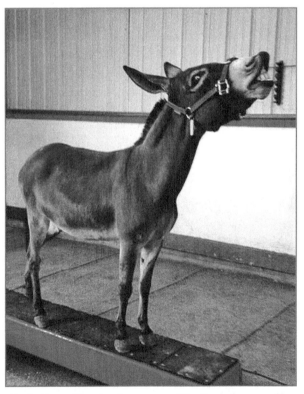

Cash Benefit, also known as Big Ben shows off his smile.

Let the horse pick the treat out of your hand. He will soon start reaching for it and extending his upper lip.

Cues
- **Vocal cue** is "Smile"
- **Proximity cue** can be very close and progress to as far away as your horse will respond.
- **Physical cue** can be to hold up your index finger.

Steps
How to Get Them Smiling

1. Hold a small treat in the palm of your hand and lightly close your fingers around it.

   Let the horse smell it and invite him to nose through your fingers as though he were picking a blade of grass. He will quickly begin to hunt the treat, which is a signal for you to move your hand back a little so he twitches his nose or reaches for the treat.

   When his upper lip moves, tell him "good boy" and immediately open your fingers and give him the treat. Encourage him to lift his lip a little higher each session and add the verbal cue of "smile."

   Add a lifted index finger so he begins to get a Visual Cue as well. Reward him with a cookie each time he responds with even a small improvement. The smile always requires a reward (quickly), each and every time or he will very soon lose interest.

2. The next step is to slowly begin to move your hand from a palm up low position to a palm forward and higher position as if saying a pledge. To get the treat, the horse has to use the lip in a prehensile way. When he consistently finds the hidden treat, begin to shape the behavior into a Smile.

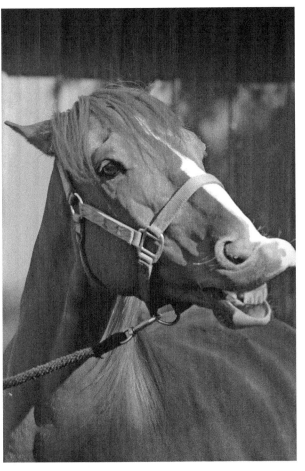

3. A Bridge Signal will instantly let him know he is offering the desired behavior and a treat is forthcoming. Use the word "Good" when you see any movement of his upper lip extending to reach the treat. As time goes on, only reward improvement in the form of an upward move of the lip in a smile-like expression.

4. To continue shaping the Smile, you can use the end of your index finger to tickle the underside of the horse's upper lip. This will encourage him to raise his lip in a way resembling the Flehmen response (horses do this when they smell something unusual or something they want to remember). Encourage the horse to hold the lip upturned even if for a fraction of a second longer each time by withholding the bridge signal momentarily. This is a great trick for your horse to think he is training you!

Slowly increase the distance from which you can stand and ask for a smile.

Common Problems

- Horses can get very pushy in demanding treats.

- Use small treats.

Tips

- Teaching the Smile on a pedestal will help keep a horse in place, minimizing pushiness for a treat.

- The Smile can be taught with stall gate between horse and handler to prevent pushiness.

- Monitor the Smile when you allow children or other handlers to cue the horse. Most casual handlers do not understand the necessity of rewarding only improvement and the horse may soon lose the Smile you have spent time honing.

- Reward him immediately with a Bridge Cue followed by the treat.

- A horse will only Smile a certain number of times without a reward.

Each horse has an individual way of smiling.

Pedestal Training

How Pedestal Training Can Improve Your Horse

Did you know virtually every species of animal trained by humans is done so with the use of a "place" or a "mark"? This applies to dolphins, big cats, dogs, birds and elephants. If you watch dog agility, you will see up close how effectively the mark is used. The dog returns to his place after completing a trick or series of moves and awaits his next cue. His place or mark is his personal space where he receives praise, a food treat or even a well-deserved time out.

In ground training, the pedestal gives a horse somewhere to go rather than just act out on his flight instinct and flee or shut down when pressure is applied. Horses have been running away from things for eons and a pedestal gives the horse a place to go to and a place to stay. **Quiet feet equal a focused mind.** Pedestal work helps to develop physical dexterity while increasing self-confidence and boldness. Ground tying, yielding of the hindquarters and many other useful lessons are taught through pedestal training. Pedestal training will help create a willing horse that will Step Up, Step Over, Step Around, Step Back on a Pedestal and trail obstacles too.

How and why does pedestal training help to instill willing obedience?

Horses love to stand on pedestals, possibly because it makes them taller than usual and higher than other horses, which increases their confidence. Standing with the front feet on a pedestal shifts the weight off the front end and helps a horse stretch and relax his back. We think this may allow the horse to find chiropractic relief or self-adjustment.

Horses of any age benefit from Pedestal Training. These fillies are two weeks old.

"End of the Trail" pose by Yellow Blanket.

Many requests made of horses in standard training surely must seem nebulous from their perspective. Take, for example, yielding the hindquarters. Why does a horse respond to the request in groundwork? He responds because he is given a release of pressure (applied by the handler) for responding correctly to the request and over time, the response becomes automatic.

Let's take the release of pressure a step further. What if a horse were to receive not only a release of pressure but also self (intrinsic) satisfaction? That's exactly what the usual outcome of pedestal training is. With his front feet anchored on a pedestal, it is easy for him to understand yielding the hindquarters because he has a reason for his front feet to stay still.

Sombra exhibits total trust in allowing Allen to show her where to place her foot.

In pedestal training, as we will demonstrate, **the trick becomes the reward.**

Goals of pedestal training include:

- Have the horse mount the pedestal with two (front) feet and then all four feet. He should stand quietly until given the release cue.

- Perform related tricks while on the pedestal or stand quietly until released.

- Give the horse a "place" that is truly his own.

- Send the horse to any pedestal requested at liberty, and expect him to remain there until released.

Benefits of Pedestal Training

A horse becomes willing to stand quietly. His attention span is increased as he learns to focus on the handler and await the next cue. Because he is allowed to rest while on the pedestal, he learns to watch the handler intently. His physical dexterity is increased, especially in variations such as all four feet up or pivoting his hindquarters around the front. He learns to pay attention to what both ends of his body are doing. When he is on a small, square pedestal with all four feet, his posture automatically creates lift of his top line and of the stomach muscles, which will be helpful in creating collection under saddle.

If Pedestal Training is introduced to a foal or adolescent horse, he will become as agile as a little goat long before the time comes for saddle and trail training.

You may also see a radical change in a horse's personality, a move toward controlled boldness and confidence.

A pedestal offers a horse a place to go to rather than resorting to his primary instinct to run.

Alyah and Hasan give a Jambette in perfect unison.

Note: Sending a horse to a pedestal is covered in the Liberty I DVD.

Pedestal Safety

Horses don't usually slip on properly designed pedestals but precautions are still advised.

The construction of a pedestal is important as the sloped sides prevent skinned cannon bones if a horse slips off the top, and rubber mats on top prevent slipping.

Square, box shaped pedestals are NOT safe for horses more than a few months of age because they tip over too easily!

Perfect Placement

Teach your horse to move and/or lift each foot (all four) separately when cued. The horse should obediently Halt, Step Back and yield each part of his body when asked. Every trail horse should have the ability to place his feet with precision on his own judgment when riding out. We want him also to place those feet with precision when engaged in ground exercises, on cue. In either scenario, response and responsibility can be achieved. Precision foot placement on cue will be helpful in trailer loading, positioning for mounting, veterinary procedures and even Equine Agility. The more skills added to a horse's education, the brighter his future and the safer you will be when you are out trail riding.

Before You Begin

Precision foot placement can begin on the flat and then progress to pedestals and the multi-tiered agility platform. We initially find it helpful for clarity to use a rubber mat on the ground as a "place" or mark when teaching foot placement. Associating specific moves with objects such as the mat helps the horse to understand your requests. Setting the horse up for success through establishing associations and routine is always a good idea and enables us to educate him with fewer repetitions, which keeps stress to a minimum.

When the horse is light and responsive to a halter, each of his four feet can be asked to move separately, either coming forward or stepping back by using the halter and the horse's nose like a rudder. This takes lots of practice for the handler but is generally easy for a horse to respond correctly. Most horses give a natural response to universal cues of body direction. It is up to the handler to understand and consistently communicate requests in a horse's natural language, in this case through guidance with the halter. When this step is mastered, it's time to move to teaching individual foot cues.

First Steps

Halt the horse on the mat and give him a few seconds of dwell time. Lightly tap his pastern as you tell him to "pick it up," "step" or whatever verbal cue you like and will use consistently. Help him take the weight off the foot you want him to lift by moving his head slightly to the opposite side. For instance, if you are cueing the right front foot, move his nose slightly to his left to help him unweight the leg you want him to lift, rebalance and give the response you request. Holding the lead short underneath the chin will give a precise touch cue to his nose. As his understanding of the touch cue grows, you can give him more length on the lead.

Proceed in this manner until he will lift either front leg when touched on the pastern. Add the vocal cue of your choice. We use "Pick it up." Do the same with each back foot. A little practice goes a long way on this type of exercise. Because we are asking for such a tiny movement, too many repetitions will be counterproductive. Three or four repetitions with even a slight move of the foot is good progress. The exercise (all four feet) can be repeated a couple of times a day in short sessions.

Adding Movement

The next step is to add movement or a step to the "Pick foot up" cue. We will teach him to move each leg either forward a step or back, with precision, on cue. For the front feet, as he picks the foot up, use the vocal cue of "Step" as you guide him very slightly forward. Even a small step initially is fine. Go slowly so he will not become confused. As time goes on, he will be able to distinguish the difference between the "Pick Foot up" cue and the "Step" cue with each of his four feet. This is the beginning of true precision.

The "Step" exercise is great when practicing trailer loading; ask for tiny steps forward and back. Responding to these requests helps take the horse's mind and thus the pressure off of the loading process as he is focusing on the cues for the steps.

Once your horse has mastered the art of Precision Foot Placement on cue, he is ready to begin "stepping up" onto a variety of pedestals and platforms, one step at a time, in response to your requests. This is the prelude to Liberty Training, in which your horse will perform these maneuvers without a lead line, responding to your voice and body position.

Be Prepared… and Patient

Be prepared to prevent your horse's initial evasions. For example, if he comes over the top of the pedestal, place it against a wall or solid fence. Be as creative with problem solving as the horse is with evasions.

Each horse learns at an individual pace. It may take a horse many repetitions or even

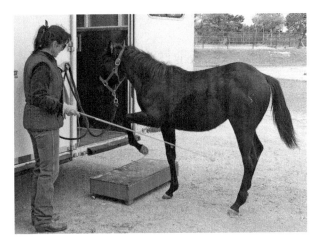

Pedestal training is mobile and makes tasks understandable.

days of repetitions before he has enough confidence to step up with both front feet. Teaching is a process, so give your horse the necessary number of repetitions and know when to stop teaching each lesson.

For mounting with two feet, approach the wide side of the rectangle pedestal. The horse will associate the wide side with the specific reason of mounting with the front feet. For mounting later on with four feet, it will be easier to approach the narrow end so the horse has room to "walk up." If using a square top pedestal, designate one side for mounting with two feet and a different side for mounting with all four feet. This helps the horse to associate which moves will be asked as he approaches each particular side.

Cue clarity

We initially use the verbal cue of "Pick it up" or "Foot" to teach the horse to yield or give each individual foot. As the pedestal training progresses, we begin to use the verbal cue of "Step Up" or simply "Up".

Cues

- Verbal cue is "Step Up" for front feet and "Walk Up" for hind feet

- Proximity cue varies

- Physical cue could be a touch on a front leg with a guider whip.

Here's How to Teach it

1. **Two Feet Up**
   Teach the horse to "Step Up" on a pedestal initially with the front feet. You may want to walk next to the horse as you approach the pedestal and later when longeing him, position yourself on the opposite side of the pedestal. During the first session (or two), it may be enough for a shy horse to just approach the pedestal and lift one foot.

   Approach the pedestal with the horse in hand and cue him to lift his front leg. It may be necessary to lift his foot up to help him place it on the pedestal. Offering the foot willingly should be a behavior that is instilled in the horse before

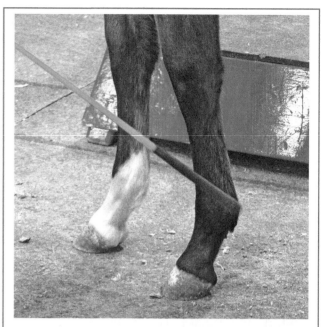

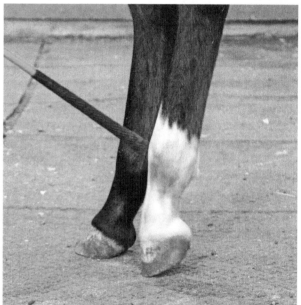

Teach a horse to pick up and move each foot separately, front and back.

It may be necessary to physically show a horse where to put his feet.

beginning. Experiment with both the handle of a dressage length whip and the snap to see which works best in asking him to lift his foot. Strive to use the mildest effective cue for each horse. A harder cue does not mean increased or quicker results and may scare the horse.

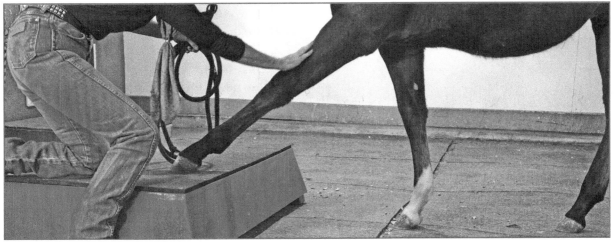
Praise the horse and stroke his leg to let him know he did what you asked.

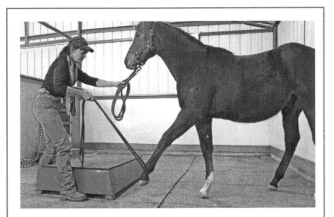

Picking up a leg with a soft cotton lead rope and placing it on the pedestal can be helpful as you begin to teach him.

Stroke the horse's leg, praise him and encourage him to leave it in place even if you lifted it into position.

Give him a release cue and ask him to step back. Take him on a walkabout and repeat the process.

Repeat this step until the horse is comfortable putting one front foot "Up" and will do it freely when asked.

Begin to encourage him to "Step Up" with both feet. Attach a lead rope and position his head over the foot that's on the pedestal. Moving his head will help him unweight the leg on the ground and make it easier for him to lift the other leg. A light flick of the schooling whip on his cannon bone can signal him to pick up the foot. Make a big fuss over

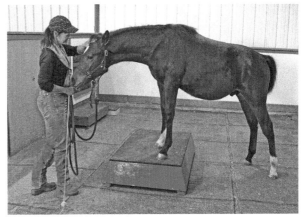
Praise each small step or try.

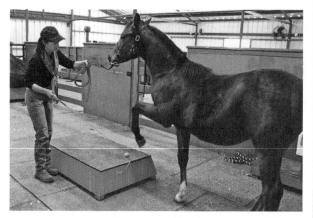

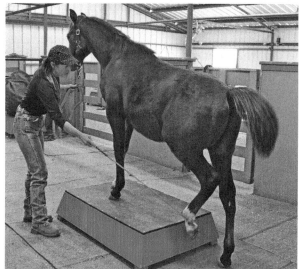

him when he steps up with both feet and reward him with a food treat.

2. **Stay**

After he will willingly step up with both front feet, encourage him to stay for incrementally longer periods of time and until he is released. Condition him to stay on the pedestal as you step back from him and walk around. This is similar to the stay command in dog training and the beginning step of Ground Tying.

The complementary and opposite part of this lesson is "Step Down." If your horse will approach the pedestal but is hesitant to mount it and you have made every step clear to him, send him off to trot circles on a working length line for a few minutes before asking him to "Try Again." Horses will understand quickly that mounting the pedestal is easier than trotting circles. If he doesn't get the picture, don't apply more pressure. Keep your cool, and each time he refuses, send him back to work on the line, with no emotion. This is not punishment; it is simply a consequence of not trying.

The horse will quickly learn he has control

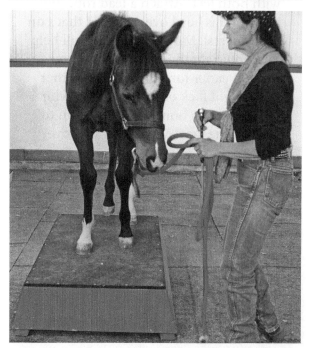

Use the wider side of a rectangular pedestal for two feet up and the narrow side for four feet up.

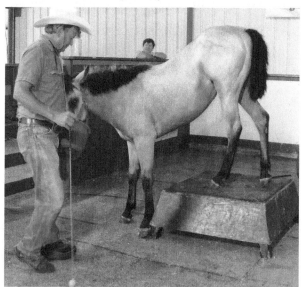

Allen is teaching this weanling a variation of pedestal work and "treating him for position."

over his work routine—he can Step Up and rest. When he mounts the pedestal, praise him and offer a food treat. Let him know he did just what you wanted. At this point the trick will have become the reward and his confidence will increase.

When on the pedestal, he will focus on the handler, as doing so seems to delay the drill of trotting circles. When he looks away, loses his focus or steps down before released, put him back to work trotting circles, with no visible emotion on your part. In your heart, continue to hold a positive visualization of success.

Step Down

Teach the horse a cue for dismounting the pedestal, such as "Step Down." He is to dismount the pedestal only when cued. If he dismounts before being given the release cue, send him back to work trotting circles for a few laps and try again. Do NOT startle the horse when you send him off. To make him fearful or nervous will defeat the purpose of sending him off to work. We want him to come back to the pedestal in a calm frame of mind.

Pusher Rocks begins his step off the pedestal.

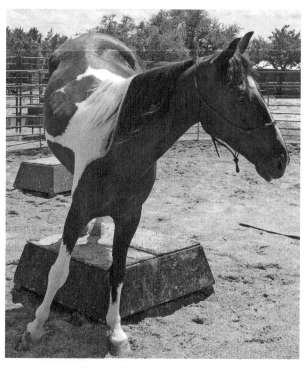

Pusher completes the revolution with only verbal cues from Sue.

Pusher completes his step and receives his reward.

Creative Challenges

When a horse is mounted on a square top pedestal with his front feet, ask him to yield the hindquarters or "Step Around" as his front feet remain on the pedestal. Gradually increase the number of side steps until he can completely circle the hindquarters around the pedestal. With his front feet anchored on the pedestal, the request will be easy for him to understand. He can also be taught to step the front feet down and walk around them while the rear feet remain on the pedestal.

The pedestal can serve as a horse's mark for executing other moves, such as the Jambette, Retrieving an Object and even a slow Spin. If two horses are worked together, teach them to Change Places in a musical chair fashion or to line up side by side on pedestals.

Horsemanship principles, tact, good judgment, a systematic approach and reasonable expectations are required. Taking time to plan will make your sessions fun and fruitful for both horse and human.

Step Around

Yielding of the hindquarters around the front end is the natural progression of pedestal work and the first step toward working on the revolving pedestal. Initially ask for only

A larger and longer pedestal or agility platform makes initial learning easier.

a step at a time and increase the number of steps gradually.

Four Feet Up

Each horse will respond differently to a request to mount with all four feet. Some horses walk right up while others will present all sorts of evasions. Some of the more common issues include:

Transferring a move to mounted work is easiest with a helper.

Variations

- Revolving pedestal

- Walk the Plank (a long, narrow, elevated pedestal)

- Multi-tiered or stair-step pedestal

- Agility Platform (multi-levels like a wedding cake)

- Large and tall pedestals

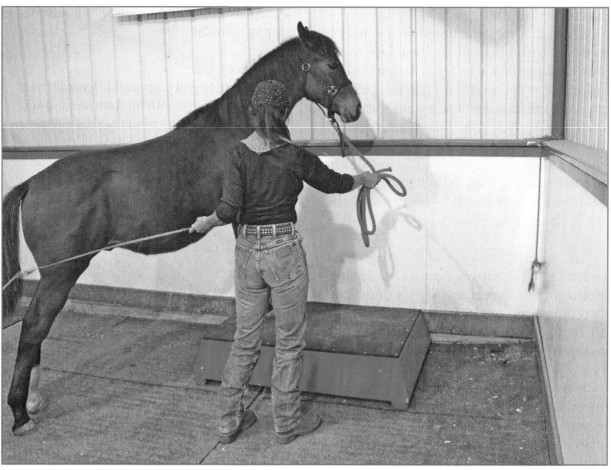

Place the pedestal in a corner to help prevent evasions.

- Pulling the feet back after you have placed them on the pedestal

- Walking around the pedestal rather than stepping up on to it

- Jumping or walking over the pedestal

- Barging over the top of a handler if he is frightened or doesn't understand the request.

To make mounting with all four feet easier, we use a low, oversized pedestal or a large Agility Platform. We want to build confidence, and asking even a willing, kind horse to step up with all four feet on a pedestal that is too small is not fair. We use big and low pedestals for training and progress to taller

and smaller tops as the horse's balance and confidence increase.

It may initially be necessary to have one handler hold the horse's head while another helper picks up the horse's hind foot and places it on the pedestal.

For a horse that evades stepping up with all four feet, place the pedestal against a wall near a corner of a stall to limit his escape options. The horse may try to escape by lunging forward or pulling back, so place the pedestal in a way that will help prevent evasion in each situation. The tendency to barge over the pedestal can also be deterred with a light flick to the tips of his ears or by putting the butt end of a whip in his shoulder muscle groove. Another method is to deflect his movement

The Trick Horse Companion

Boullet learns to work the agility platform, step by step.

by giving him a firm push on the soft part of his nose to help him change his direction.

Pedestal Training Tips

- Teach a horse to pick up each individual foot on cue. This can be done by lightly tapping the lower cannon bone with a whip or light bamboo cane. (A bamboo cane gives a very light touch and is often more effective than a commercial whip.) When he lifts the leg, immediately quit tapping and praise him.

- If your horse evades a pedestal in the open, place it in a corner or along a wall.

- Teach the horse to "Whoa" prior to pedestal training to help prevent him from coming off the pedestal into your space.

- If your horse won't keep his foot on the pedestal initially, put a hobble and lead rope on one front foot and ask an assistant to help hold it in place. The helper should stand on the opposite side of the pedestal from the horse to help lift the foot with the hobble rope and move it forward and onto the pedestal. Hold the foot in place with the rope as you ask the horse to step up with the second foot. This simple fix is often enough to increase the horse's cooperation and confidence.

- When the horse understands where the pedestal is in relation to his front feet, stepping the back feet up is usually easy.
- Reward each honest try.

- For serious evasions and disobedi-

Teach the horse to take one step at a time, carefully, and not to leap.

ence, go back to basic groundwork. DO NOT punish or hit the horse, especially on the head, for any reason. This is a very callous action and the horse's eye could be an accidental target.

Working Into Pressure on the Pedestal

Corners of a square pen or large schooling stall can be used to teach a unique concept we call "working into pressure." This is different than teaching a horse to physically move away from pressure. Working into pressure enhances boldness while creating obedience. The horse will learn to think, to comprehend your intention and then to act appropriately, not merely react and run away.

The horse should know pedestal basics before moving to Working into Pressure. If he has been taught to mount the pedestal with at least the two front feet, place it at an angle in the corner of the pen, five to six feet from where the two sides meet. Ask the horse (at liberty if possible) to trot into the corner and "turn" toward you. Motivate him to hustle and as he turns toward you, step back and ask him to Step Up, facing you. As he steps up, you will simultaneously give him space and lower both whips, releasing him of the pressure of your proximity and physical stance.

Turning toward you and stepping up must be presented to him as his only option, the only way the pressure on him will be released. During the first few repetitions, if he doesn't understand the request or is nervous, lead him to the pedestal and ask him to "Step Up" to demonstrate your request and then proceed. Two whips are necessary to block both escape paths along the walls. The whips are held horizontally and slightly higher than his eye level to block his escape. Immediately lower and relax your arms, drop the whip tips to the ground as he takes a step toward the pedestal (to step up). This helps him to understand his release.

Sending the Horse to a Pedestal

When the horse will work into pressure and step up on the pedestal as he comes toward you, he is ready to learn to be "sent" to a pedestal. It is similar to working into pressure but the horse may not be moving toward you when he steps up or mounts the pedestal. This variation is the solution for the common problem of a horse that will step up but then "quits," steps down or moves away.

Begin with one pedestal situated five to seven feet from the perimeter of a small round pen. Ask the horse to make several calm circles of the ring and as he approaches the pedestal, step slightly in his path and cue him to step up. If necessary, use the long longe whip to reach around and touch his rump. The guider whip can be held upright to help limit his forward motion and guide him to line up with the pedestal.

It is important to be insistent in your request and not accept evasions. He may dodge and turn in an attempt to evade, which is why we use two whips to keep him on track.

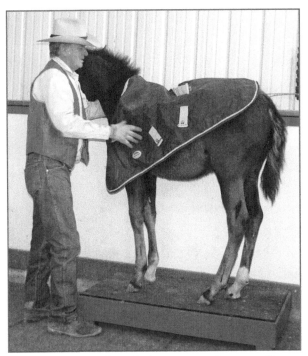

The familiar pedestal gives youngsters confidence to learn about new objects and skills.

Your position will help him to submit and comply with your request. You will control the ground he wishes to cover and make his only option for release (piece of real estate) the pedestal.

This can be achieved using a rubber mat designated as his place. We begin by placing it near the center of the ring and teach a horse to come in from the perimeter and stand with his front feet (to begin with) on the mat.

In time the mat can be moved to encourage the horse to go to or come to any position you desire.

Further instructions are included in the DVD *"Pedestal Training."*

The Jambette

Many of the poses we teach are versions of moves horses already do on their own—we simply coach them to perform on cue. As with human athletes, extreme poses and stretches will give extreme benefits. If there is any doubt horses stretch in extreme manners on their own, just watch a horse practically stand on his head to reach under a fence for a few bites of green grass or young horses posturing for herd position as they challenge each other with their front legs.

A nice Jambette by Athena, a Tennessee Walking Horse filly.

In classical French training, the Leg Extension or Salute is called the Jambette. We teach it at the Halt, on a pedestal, then add forward movement and mold it in time into the Spanish Walk.

The Jambette is usually fun for the horse because most love to kick out with the front feet. This makes teaching the Jambette a great opportunity to help him understand correct vs. incorrect response without becoming discouraged. He will easily understand praise for offering it correctly and will take correction without becoming discouraged if he offers the wrong leg. Differentiating the leg cues will be helpful later on in teaching the Spanish Walk.

The Jambette can be taught on the ground, but we prefer to teach it in association with a pedestal. A finished exhibition horse may know half a dozen moves that begin with a slightly different cue on his front legs. Using a pedestal in association with teaching the Jambette helps to ensure the horse will offer the move only on cue, while on the pedestal and not unexpectedly, especially in the initial stages of training.

Equipment

A Pedestal and a dressage-length whip are the basics. *If the Spanish Walk is the goal, a cleat board is a must-have tool.* A cleat board is easy to build and will help a horse to develop an exceptionally long reach with his front leg.

The cleat board is similar to the barre that humans use for balance in a dance studio and a great help in teaching the Jambette. Targeting the cleat board will help a horse develop the extension needed to move from a Jambette to the beginning of a Spanish Walk.

The cleat board is a half sheet of ¾-inch

plywood with thick, horizontal wooden cleats. Attach it securely to a wall or strong fence with screws or bolts. The cleats are made from rounded 4 x 4s or landscape timbers and arranged like the rungs of a ladder starting about knee high and approximately

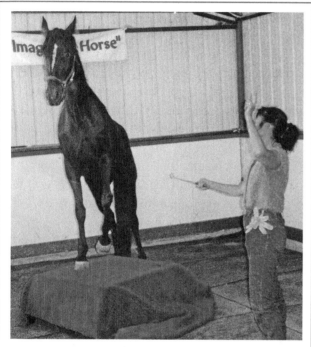

Touch or tap the horse's leg and ask her to move or lift it. Stand on the side that you want the horse to lift.

10 to 12 inches apart. It should be positioned so the path of approach (horse and handler's) is parallel to a wall to keep the horse moving in a straight line.

Goals

- A full extension of the leg with the knee joint flat

- First step to teaching the Spanish Walk

Benefits

- Strengthen and develop range of motion in a horse's shoulder, front legs and back

- Because most horses love to strike out with their legs, they can take correction without becoming discouraged

- Teaches right from left, and right (response) from wrong (response)

Cues

Verbal Cue could be "Salute," "Hello" or whatever you like best. If you plan to teach the Spanish Walk, consider cadence cues such as "One" for the left leg and "Two" for the right front leg.

Proximity Cue is usually (to stand) in front of and to the side of the horse's left shoulder for the left leg and to the right for the right leg. If the horse is on a pedestal, stand on the opposite side of it. In cueing the horse for a left leg lift, hold the guider whip in the right hand and lift your left arm in the air. Your arm will stay in the air as a cue until the horse is released. This can be done by lowering your arm.

Physical Cue is a touch on the horse's leg, usually behind the forearm, point of the shoulder or at the back of the knee. You will have to discover the touch each horse responds to best.

Jambette Tips

- Most horses enjoy doing the Jambette, but the quick reach and stretch could be inadvertently cued by a child, so consider this when teaching it.

- Keep out of range of the horse's front legs to avoid an accidental strike.

- As the horse becomes confirmed in giving the correct leg on cue, ask for bigger lifts and progressively longer hold periods.

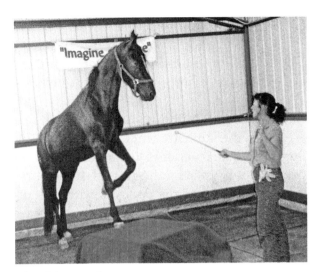

Ask for and reward improvement every time you work with your horse.

- Be certain the horse thoroughly understands your request from one side before moving to the opposite side.

- Three repetitions per lesson are

Illusion offers a good reach in the second session.

plenty; be sure to include "walkabout time" before continuing.

- Reward only improvements in lift and reach.

- To discourage repeated pawing or giving the incorrect leg, quickly reward the first reach and look away from the horse and ignore further pawing or walk away and leave him alone for 5 or 10 minutes.

- Teach the Jambette on a pedestal, as it decreases the chance the horse will offer a salute unsolicited on the ground.

- Adjust your proximity to the horse when cueing each separate leg.

- We use "One" as the verbal cue for the left and "Two" as the cue for the right leg. These verbal cues help us to count cadence and encourage the horse to lift the legs in the correct sequence for the Spanish Walk.

- All horses will assuredly offer the incorrect leg in the beginning.

• The withdrawal of a reward or possibility of a reward has a profound effect on a horse's willingness to work.

Jambette on the Pedestal

Teach the Jambette while a horse is standing with his front feet on a pedestal, not when standing flat on the ground. If the horse learns to associate the pedestal with executing the Jambette, you will greatly reduce the likelihood of accidentally striking a person with a foot.

Step the horse up onto the pedestal with his front feet. Stand on the near or left side of the horse, with the lead in the left hand, a dressage or guider whip in the right hand. Tap the horse lightly just behind the knee until he offers even a slight movement of the leg. Keep the touch a light flick as a harder touch will not be any easier for the horse to understand and may actually hinder his understanding of the request.

Even if he only offers a few inches of lift, praise and give him a few seconds to understand that he offered the correct response. Reward each try with praise and a stroke on the neck and a few seconds of dwell time between each repetition. As he progresses, reward only for improvement.

We generally teach the leg lift on the left

Navegador and Rafiq give a perfectly synchronized double Salute.

side until the horse is accurate and reliable in offering his leg before we teach it on the right side.

The handler's body position will be reversed or moved to the right side in teaching the horse to lift his right leg.

Cleat Board

"Targeting" an object is generally done by teaching a horse to touch the object with his nose in order to get a treat, but in this case he will target with his foot. Targeting can be used to reduce fear of objects as the horse always receives a reward in association with touching the object.

A specific request, such as placing a foot on the cleat board, leaves no gray area for a horse to interpret. When expectations are clear to a horse, he will begin to want to respond, which signifies the beginning of a real work ethic.

Horses seem to enjoy flexing their entire shoulder, base of the neck and leg muscles once they become confident in reaching for the cleat board. Some horses become infatuated with the opportunity to kick at the cleats, which is remedied by teaching the opposite.

A tense or nervous horse will tend to raise the knee then pull back or contract the lower leg. This is a defensive posture indicating he either lacks confidence or physical relaxation.

The goal is to get the horse to completely relax and straighten the leg by flattening the knee joint. You can hold the hoof in your hand and gently stretch his leg forward to flatten the knee and raise it little by little. Reward your horse for allowing you to manipulate his leg in this way.

You'll need to distinguish the correct distance for your horse to stand from the board to be able to reach it. Walk the horse to the cleat board and cue him for the leg lift on whichever side you choose. Most horses require help at first to place a foot on the rung. We usually pick up the foot and physically place it on the lowest rung, stretching and balancing it across our thigh to help support it.

Tapping the horse's toe against the cleat or plywood backboard seems to make the request more obvious. Some horses will try to pull the leg back; continue to support the leg while stroking it and offering a treat for the position.

If a horse is insistent in pulling the leg back, pick it up and try again. With a little practice and praise or a food reward, most horses quickly learn to reach out and balance a foot on the rung. Using the lower rungs of the cleat board makes it easy for the horse to acclimate to the stretch required for the higher cleats.

Reverse your proximity to work with the opposite leg. If taught correctly, the horse can be cued from either side and accurately place the respective leg on a rung of the cleat board. When he will put either leg on a rung, position him three or four steps back from the

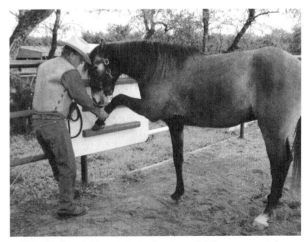

Allen helped Uno to understand his request by helping him place his foot on the rung.

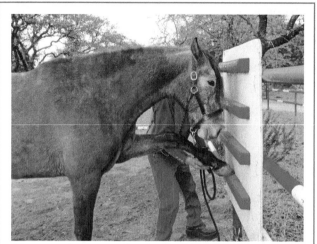

You may have to physically lift the horse's leg to the target board to show him what you are asking.

Some horses respond better to the touch of a light bamboo cane rather than a flexible whip.

Further instructions are included in the DVD *"Shaping Behaviors I".*

cleat board, walk him forward and cue him to reach for the target with each step. Draw a line on the floor (in front of the cleat board) to position the horse accurately each time you ask him to move forward with a leg extension. If he is too far back, he cannot reach the cleat; if he is too close, he will not be able to stretch his leg straight. He will try to reach the cleat even if he is too far away, which is how the Spanish Walk evolves.

Marz, a weanling, reaches for the target board while cued from a distance.

The first step in transferring to mounted work in preparation for the Spanish Walk.

The Trick Horse Companion

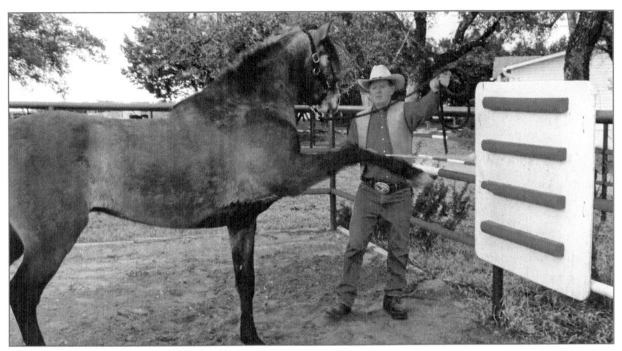

When the horse can be cued to put either leg on the board, back him a few steps from it and ask him to reach for it as he walks.

Pusher has achieved a good lift even when cued from afar.

A variation of the Jambette is a cocked leg salute.

The Trick Horse Companion

Tricks of Trust

Building the Spirit of Compliance

The Obeisance, Kneel, Bow and Lie Down

A generous and compliant spirit makes a trail horse or companion horse a joy to be with, yet the essence of compliance is a little difficult to describe. Compliance isn't exactly obedience nor is it submission, yet it is a step *beyond* cooperation. The dictionary says compliance means to *acquiesce*, or give readily to others. On the equine terminology scale, it may be best described as "agreeing to be agreeable" on the part of the horse. Building the spirit of compliance requires the artful application of equestrian tact, which yields the desired response from the horse while preserving his good will. Compliance will manifest in many ways in the relationship between human leader and equine student and can be gained in many diverse ways.

One of the methods we use to build willing obedience is teaching "Tricks of Trust." These are moves or poses requiring the horse to lower his body and his eye in relation to the handler's, which puts him in a naturally and instinctually vulnerable position. Tricks of Trust include the Obeisance, Bow, Kneel and Lie Down. Learning these moves will teach a horse to accept a physical and mental attitude of self-restraint, which leads to trusting compliance.

There are many practical reasons to use lessons of restraint in horse training; veterinary treatment and panic situations top the list. Make no mistake about it—many unforeseen incidents can happen on even a casual trail ride within a couple of miles of home!

A horse's life may literally depend on whether or not he can be restrained until help can be summoned.

In his book, *"Understanding the Ancient Secrets of the Horse's Mind,"* Dr. Robert M. Miller says of horses, "They are naturally flighty creatures, but the flight response can be quickly extinguished so long as they are not hurt. Thus, with the correct training techniques, horses can be taught to overcome the claustrophobia of confinement. Once horses accept the confinement of a saddle, hobbles, a stake rope, a stall or anything else that inhibits escape, they develop a more subordinate attitude. This means they are more accepting of leadership, more reliant upon human guidance and more willing to work together with us."

Why We Use Hobble Training to Gain Trust

We use Hobble Training as a first step in preparing a horse for learning Tricks of Trust but it is a lesson of its own in physical AND mental restraint and self-control and can be beneficial in veterinary treatment or restraint. We teach all of our horses to quietly and confidently accept hobbles as well as a soft rope looped around the pasterns. This is hobble training basics for the purpose of learning specific moves and poses and is different than hobble training for purposes of controlling grazing.

In teaching a horse restraint of any kind, including hobble use, *it is the handler who is earning the horse's trust,* not *the horse earning the handler's trust!* Compliance follows trust. The welfare of the horse—mentally, physically and emotionally—is of the utmost importance.

Wrap each leg with two or three polo wraps in a criss cross pattern beginning above the knee and ending mid-cannon bone.

We consider these aspects carefully and may vary our approach slightly for each horse; in other words, know your horse and his learning capabilities, including his emotional capacity!

Considerations Before Introducing Hobbles

- If a horse has basic fears or behavioral issues, you'll want to solve them before moving on to hobble training or Tricks of Compliance.

- When introducing any new equipment, use incremental and easy to understand lessons.

- School the horse in the same location until his response pattern is consistent.

- Prepare yourself mentally to have a positive attitude about hobble training. Always be relaxed, respectful and non-confrontational with your horse.

Preparation for Success

Use only well-made hobbles lined with real sheepskin or thick felt. Manmade sheepskin lining is really not adequate and neither are unlined hobbles. Provide leg protection for the horse, including several polo wraps for each leg and soft footing. Start the polo wrap above the knee, use a crisscross pattern with the polo wraps over the knee and complete the wrapping below the knee on the cannon bone. Use at least two wraps on each leg. You cannot be too careful with your horse's legs!

We recommend modifying shipping boots with added padding. This sounds odd, but when you place the shipping boots on upside

Place the hobble on the leg that you will ask the horse to lift.

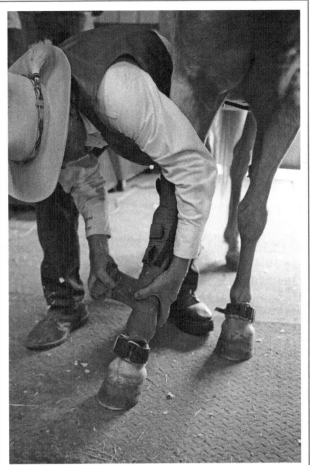

If you plan to go on to the Lie Down, you may want to wrap the leg completely or even add shipping boots over the polo wraps. The shipping boots should be put on upside down and backwards (the Velcro fasteners on the outside of the leg).

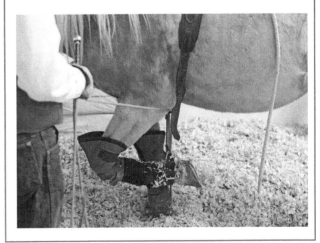

down and backwards over the horse's knee they fit and flex better (for this purpose). The boot can be anchored in place if needed with a polo wrap that covers the horse's fetlock and the lower part of the boot.

Deep shavings are a good footing for teaching a horse about hobbles. Sand, even if it is deep, is harsh and abrasive to the horse's skin and can stick to the sheepskin on the hobbles and grind away hair and flesh. We have used sand for a one-time photo shoot, but not to train in!

You will need a slide rope 12-to-14 feet long of small diameter with a small snap on one end. The rope should be rather slick so it will slide easily in the D-rings of the surcingle bellyband and not stick. Climbing rope or sailboat rope has a lively feel ("body") to it and a nice grip. It needs to be long enough to create the full Running W rigging but not so long that you have a lot of extra length to deal with.

Many tack stores and catalogs carry leather surcingles, and a saddle maker or leather shop can make one for you. The bellyband needs to have three D-rings sewn and riveted in, and it should be lined with sheepskin. If you would like to order them from our maker, Beverly McCord, contact us through our website listed elsewhere in this book.

Teaching the Horse About Hobbles

Introduce hobbles by placing one on the horse's front leg and leading him around; if he is quiet, let him stand tied with it on. Don't leave him unattended while introducing new equipment.

It is a good idea to teach the horse to pick up each foot when cued before going on to ask him to give it with the rope rigging on.

With the surcingle in place, snap the 12-to-14 foot slide rope to the middle D-ring in the belly band, run it down and through the left hobble ring, then back up and through the near (left) D-ring on the belly band and finally, to your hand. Ask the horse to lift the left leg as you cue him with the tap of a guider whip and add a verbal cue if you like, such as "Give me your foot."

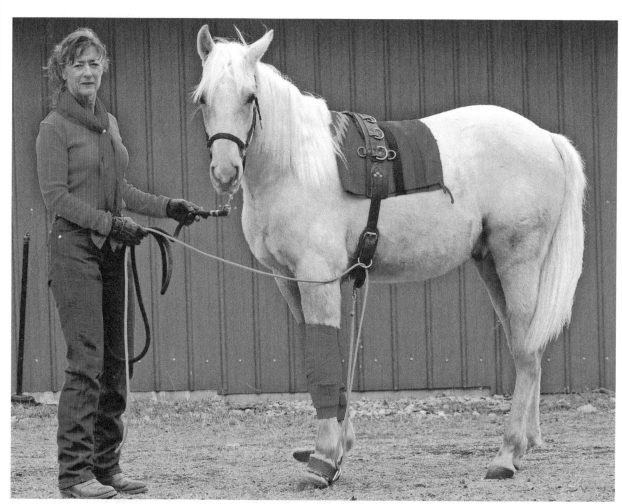

Boullet is fully rigged with leg wraps, hobbles, surcingle and pull rope.

Stand next to him, facing his head before you ask for a leg.

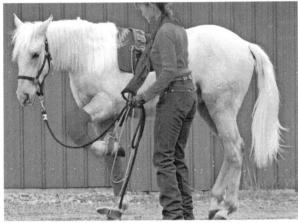

Lift the horse's leg for only a few seconds at first and give it back to him quickly.

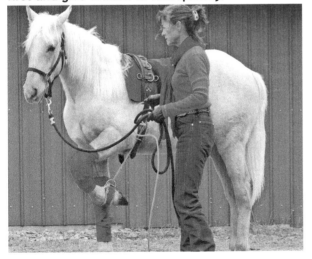

Add a verbal cue such as "down" or "ok" as you release his leg as dropping it abruptly could surprise him.

When he lifts the leg, hold it up for only a second or two with the rope before letting him put it down. Some horses don't mind at all when the leg is lifted and other horses will take multiple sessions to become comfortable with the leg being held up.

The horse may hop around; this is normal. Your confidence should tell the horse he has nothing to fear. Praise him each time he willingly lets his leg be lifted. The lesson is the release of his leg, not in retaining control of it. If you use food treats, be sure to offer one while his leg is up and not after he puts it down. This is "treating for position."

Increase the time you hold his leg up with each repetition within his comfort level. It usually only takes a few lessons before the horse understands you can be trusted to give his leg back in a reasonable amount of time. The lesson is he can trust you.

After the leg lift is confirmed on the left side, teach the same lesson from the "off" or right side of the horse. Be sure to reverse your position and the rigging too.

When the horse understands and is comfortable with the leg lift and hold exercise, begin teaching him to shift his weight to his hindquarters. This change of balance begins to prepare the horse for the weight shifts required to Kneel, Bow and Lie Down. The weight shift exercise can be done by encouraging him to take a step or two to the side (either) with just three legs while holding up a leg with the hobble. Don't over-do this exercise, as it is a lesson in trust, balance and confidence.

Further instructions on hobble training are included in the DVDs *Trick Training Fundamentals I and II*.

The Trick Horse Companion

The Obeisance

Horses may naturally perform an obeisance position while stretching, rising from a nap or lowering the body to reach for a bite of grass under a fence. They may also give this stretch completely for reasons we will never know.

Obeisance (pronounced o-bay-sans) means a position of supreme submission.

This is a submissive position to a horse because his body is lowered, which puts him (as is his nature) in an instinctually vulnerable position.

He is our partner and it is very important to preserve his spirit and good will and to treat these always as assets. Learning the Obeisance increases his trust and confidence in the handler, especially if he receives sufficient praise.

The Obeisance involves virtually every muscle in a horse's body from nose to tail as evidenced in the rounded curves of the top line while in the pose. A horse's front legs are stretched out in front of his body and are more or less straight, the nose is tucked back and between the front legs and the entire front end of the horse is lowered. A horse often will learn to walk his back legs out behind him in order to make lowering his body easier. We can help the horse by teaching him the Park Out prior to the Obeisance as it helps him to walk his hind legs out behind him.

Navegador executes a lovely Obeisance.

The Obeisance prepares the horse physically and mentally for the Bow, Kneel and Lie Down.

Equipment

- Gloves
- Guider or other short whip to tap the belly as a cue
- Food treats—long slivers only

Goals

- Lowering of the body and stretching out the front legs, walking the back legs out behind the body
- Stay down until given a "Release" cue

Benefits

- A stretching and gymnastic exercise engaging nearly every muscle in the horse's body
- Expressed submission and trust by a horse

Cues

Verbal cue could be "Pretty Down" or "Stretch"

Proximity cue is usually next to the horse's left shoulder Lower your body slightly to go with the motion required of the horse

Physical cue is usually to tap the under side of the horse's belly with the butt of a whip

Steps

Yes, it is necessary to lure the horse into position during the initial stages of training. Ducking for a treat is not the trick, staying until released is the trick. Wear gloves!

Stand at the left side of the horse and place your right hand on the near side of his withers while leaning slightly into him with your arm extended. The intent is to help him remove the weight (un-weight) from his nearside leg.

Place your foot behind his near pastern

and with your toe, position his front foot slightly forward and out to the side to make room for his head to fit between his legs.

Each step of this process should be considered a separate or individual trick. Proceed at your horse's understanding level before moving ahead.

When he moves his left foot to the side as asked and your right hand remains on his withers, lightly tap his belly twice with the handle of a whip or soft wand held in your left hand. This is an additional cue that will be used later to ask for the Obeisance while mounted.

While his left leg is extended, use a food treat and ask him to follow it toward his chest before giving it to him. In following repetitions, gradually reposition the treat so he follows it down and back between his front legs. Be sure to wear gloves as some horses get greedy and will snap at a treat and may accidentally grab a finger. Grabbing or snapping for the treat usually diminishes as the horse becomes more confident.

Gradually reposition the treat so he follows it down and back between his front legs. Entice him to follow the treat rather than just to duck and grab it. Muscle memory and strength must be developed over time for this extreme pose and should not be hurried or forced onto the horse. He should be praised appropriately.

As his ability to reach and stretch grows, gradually lower the treat down and back between his front legs and encourage him to stay down for incrementally longer periods of time.

Sue placed her foot behind Deano's left front foot to move it to the side as she said "Ready?"

Sue combined moving his left foot with placing her right hand on his withers as she pushed lightly to let him know know to shift his weight to the right or in other words, unweight the left foot.

In two or three sessions Deano had learned to follow the treat down and between his front legs.

To increase his eagerness, try holding several treats in the palm of your hand and offer them one at a time while he remains in position.

Encourage and praise him while he is lowering his body to let him know he is responding correctly. Add a stay cue such as "Whoa" to encourage him to remain in position. Increase the hold time gradually and expect only a small improvement with each session.

When the horse is reliable at holding the Obeisance, the food treats can be delayed until the horse is released to rise.

Proceed to the point he will execute the pose and take a treat after he is released and rises. The bridge signal "Good" can be added to help him understand a treat is coming. Most horses adjust easily to this slight change in receiving a food reward.

If a horse yields to the bit, you may help him to stay down longer or until released by placing the reins (together) between his front legs. Encourage him with a very light touch to stay down until you release him. This will work only if a horse is not claustrophobic. The act of ducking down and then immediately popping up is of no value in creating a beautiful and beneficial Obeisance. The slow, progressive act of lowering the entire front of the body and then rising on cue (release) is what we are seeking.

This is a great position although Deano had not yet learned to walk his back legs out to make it easier for him to get low.

If a horse is prone to knuckling over at the fetlock, try putting him on a pedestal as it changes the angle of his legs.

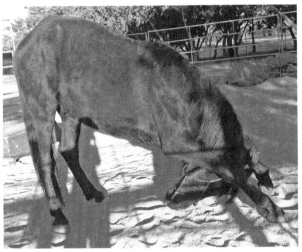

This horse will be able to get lower when he learns to walk his back legs out behind him.

Teaching a horse the Park Out position will make it easier for him to lower his body.

It is beneficial and relevant to ask him for an Obeisance prior to feeding. In this manner, the horse's ration becomes the reward rather

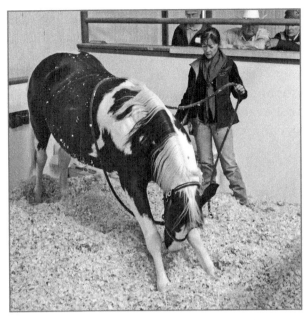

A lead rope run between Lady C's front legs, over her back and into Sue's hand encourages her to stay down even though it is slack.

than handheld treats. When asking for the Obeisance at feeding time, use a half-sized bucket and introduce the bucket by giving him a nibble of feed from your hand. When the horse is in the Obeisance position, give him the Release cue and when he rises quickly put the bucket under his nose. This is the sequence to transfer the reward for the completion of the trick.

Dick Wallen's Method

Our friend Dick Wallen grew up in the 1930s learning horse training from his father Harry Wallen. He was drafted into service during World War II and served as a cook in Italy, where he bought a donkey from a local farmer for $10. He taught the donkey some tricks to entertain himself and his friends and was seen by an officer in the USO who recruited Dick to transfer out of his battalion and travel entertaining the troops.

As the war ended he was called upon to help care for German horses seized as war booty and was able to smuggle the donkey on a plane that carried it back to a remount station in the United States. The Army had no use for donkeys and so he was able to purchase it and took it home when mustered out. Dick credits that trick-trained donkey for not only keeping him out of the battle zones and probably saving his life but also for feeding his growing family for several years.

The father of 12 children, six who became professional horse trainers, the Wallen family competed very successfully in five-gaited Saddle Horse competitions that were popular in the 1950s and 60s, garnering many national

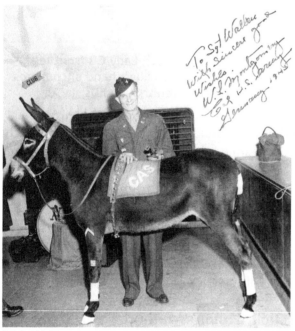

Dick Wallen

titles. At his stable in Sioux City, Iowa, Dick has hosted an annual judged competition for 'High School' horses for 60 years.

He has been the lead trainer for the Shriner's White Horse troop and now in his nineties is still teaching people and training a zebra foal. Dick is best known for a series of white Saddlebred horses all named Silver Flash (I through V), who have been performing at places like the Dixie Stampede and the Dollywood theme park.

Dick's method is for horses who will assume a low Obeisance when lured into position but then pop right back up. We must cure the pop-up immediately or it may become a confirmed evasion. This method will require an assistant, preferably a person you have worked with and communicate with well.

Before you begin, your horse should respond well to the "Whoa" signal. If he is accustomed to a snaffle bit and will yield softly, proceed as follows. Never use a curb bit for this lesson.

Bridle the horse in a snaffle bit and attach a pair of 12- to 16-foot long, light 3/8" ropes, one to each bit ring. Bring the near (left) side rope just behind the left leg at the horse's elbow and pass it under the horse's belly, up the opposite side and over the top of the back. The rope will now be on the left side of the horse. Repeat this configuration with the right (far) side rope.

Both handlers will, at the same time, take the slack out of both ropes and a put slight tension on the bit. Hold the tension, but DO NOT FORCE IT. Hold and wait for the horse to seek relief from it by either tucking his nose or better yet rocking back with the shoulders. If he gives even a fraction of an inch, release both ropes immediately with an exaggerated release of the ropes over his back. The release is the reward and indicates to the horse he has done the right thing.

Most horses will respond to this method with little resistance after they discover how to relieve the tension of the rope by yielding. Do not try to rush the progress as this is an extreme pose and may make the horse feel slightly claustrophobic.

The ropes should not be used strictly for leverage or control but to influence the horse to yield. A horse must be allowed to respond at his own pace and of course with equestrian tact on your part.

Most horses figure this method out quickly, although we had several horses resist and resent it. We switched to slipping the reins between the horse's front legs and made great progress with no resentment from the horses.

Common Problems

- It is easy for the horse to accidentally grab your fingers, as he cannot see them when you're holding a treat under his belly

- Bending the legs at the knees and knuckling over at the fetlocks

- Most horses will pop up quickly until taught to wait for a "release" cue

- Snatching or grabbing for the treat

- Resists stretching down

Tips

- Use long slivers of carrots (not chunks) to help prevent the horse from biting your fingers!

- Knuckling over at the fetlock joint will usually cease as a horse develops balance.

- If a horse continues to knuckle over or roll his ankles, put a hobble and lead rope on the foot and have an assistant hold it in place (from the front) to help the horse extend it properly.

- Harder/stronger cues do not result in escalated results and can squelch a horse's desire to try.

- Incremental improvements vary greatly from horse to horse.

- Use a stick or end of a broken whip to impale a small chunk of carrot so you can maintain an upright position.

- Some horses learn the Obeisance in a few tries and some will take up to several weeks.

- When the Obeisance is confirmed using a treat, ask for it before giving a regular meal in the morning. A hungry horse will offer a very snappy execution of most tricks.

- Run a lead on the horse's halter between his front legs and over the base of the withers from the off side to the handler's hand and apply light pressure to help the horse to stay in position.

- Teach a horse to hold the position by using the bridle method.

- Be patient and don't expect full expression too quickly. Pushing a horse even if he seems to understand the sequence may squelch his willingness to repeat the process in the coming days' sessions. This is an extreme stretch!

Further instructions are included in the DVD "*Trick Training Fundamentals I*"

The Trick Horse Companion

Preparation for Success

Tricks of Trust

Teaching the Bow, Kneel, Lie Down, Sit Up and Sit Down require proper preparation for the training area. This is for the safety and comfort of the horse, which expedites learning.

Instructions for all Tricks of Trust will call for either an outdoor Lie Down area or an indoor Training or Lie Down stall.

Deep shavings should be used for teaching these tricks. We use two designated Lie Down areas: one outdoors and one inside our trick barn. The outdoor area is a large, deep mound of shavings, used bedding and old hay or straw. It does not need to be as clean or sterile as an indoor stall. The area should be large and fenced such as a paddock so a horse could not escape if he were to pull free from the handler. Having other horses housed in the area is fine as long as they do not interfere with the proceedings. If they are inquisitive and get too close, tie them while working in the area. As mentioned in the section about hobbles, be sure to avoid sand, as it is too abrasive and can damage your horse's skin and coat.

The indoor Lie Down stall should have as many as 20 to 30 bags of shavings in it. We want it to be an inviting area so a horse would naturally want to lie down in it. The shavings we use are large flake as they last longer and don't compress easily. The shavings in the stall will last a long time and can be shaped and re-shaped in training many moves. We sprinkle them with water when they seem dusty.

A leather surcingle is required for the Bow, Kneel and Lie Down. It must have a bellyband with three D-rings sewn and also riveted into it and lined with sheepskin. The buckles should not extend beyond the sheepskin lining as they could pinch the tender skin in the girth area.

As mentioned above, use only well made hobbles with real sheepskin or thick felt lining. Manmade sheepskin lining on hobbles is not adequate and neither are unlined hobbles. Provide leg protection for the horse, including several polo wraps for each leg. Start the polo wrap above the knee, use a crisscross pattern over the knee and complete the wrapping below the knee to mid cannon bone. Use at least two wraps on each leg, as you cannot be too careful with your horse's legs!

We use shipping boots for added padding. When the shipping boots are put on upside down and backwards over the horse's knee they fit and flex better (for this purpose). The boot can be anchored in place if needed with a polo wrap covering the horse's fetlock and the lower part of the boot.

You will also need a small diameter slide rope that has a lively feel in your hands. We like climbing rope or sailboat rope with a small snap tied or sewn on one end. The rope should be rather slick so that it will slide easily in the D-rings of the surcingle bellyband and not stick. It needs to be long enough to create a full Running W rigging but not so long that you have a lot of extra length to deal with.

The Trick Horse Companion

The Bow

The Obeisance is a preliminary move for the Bow and Kneel because it teaches a horse how to lower his body and balance on all four legs before we ask him to balance on just three.

Many handlers get in a hurry to teach the Bow. If it is taught before the Obeisance the horse has a hard time going back and learning the proper sequence. We've seen the Bow taught several different ways but we only use our surcingle method as it provides understanding to the horse and helps him balance as he learns.

Using the rigging is much safer for the handler, unlike methods requiring him to lift the horse's leg with his hands. The rigging allows the handler to gradually increase the distance he stands from the horse to cue for the Bow while helping the horse stay in position until released. This cannot be accomplished with other methods.

We do not want to force a horse into position as it will be counterproductive in maintaining his good will. If he has been taught each tiny step of the process and rewarded for incremental improvement, force is not necessary. The rigging gives a pulley effect to make lifting and holding the horse's leg easy for you and difficult for a horse to effectively resist. As the horse gains confidence and understanding, the rigging serves as a balance point for him.

Lady C gives a perfect Bow at liberty. Note presence of protective polo wraps on front legs.

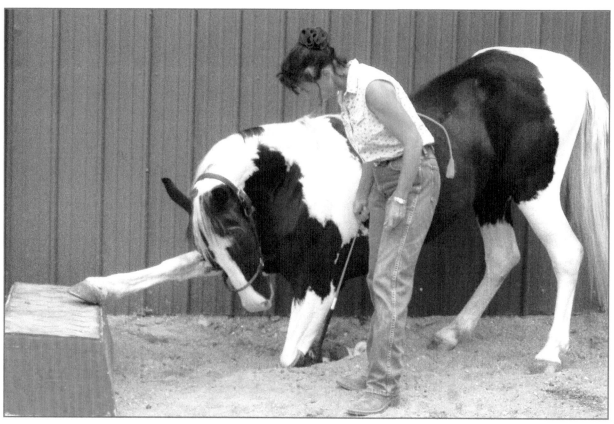

An extreme stretch helps to develop strength and range of motion.

Equipment

- Gloves

- Hobbles

- Rope—small diameter with a small snap on one end

- Polo wraps for front legs, shipping boots optional

- Halter and lead rope

- Bridle with a snaffle bit

Beginning rigging for the Bow includes polo wraps on each leg, a hobble, surcingle with belly band, pull rope. The pull rope forms a "V" as it is clipped on the middle ring of the belly band, through the hobble loop and up through the near side ring of the belly band.

Dos and Navegador take a double Bow at liberty.

Benefits

- Helps to perfect obedience and a compliant, submissive attitude in a horse

- Prepares the horse mentally and physically to learn the Kneel and Lie Down.

Cues

- **Vocal cue** is "Bow"

- **Proximity cue** is usually next to the horse's left shoulder, facing the front of the horse

- **Physical cue** can be a tap or touch on the cannon bone

Steps

1. The horse should already lift each leg on cue.

2. Rig the horse with the leg wraps, hobbles and surcingle and position him along the wall of the Lie Down stall or the outside Lie Down shavings pile. Clip the hobble rope to the center ring on the belly band, run it down through the ring on the left

hobble and back up through the nearside ring on the belly band and carry it to your hand. This forms a Running V, or one-legged rigging.

3. Cue him to lift his left leg as you quietly and gently take up the slack in the rope and hold the leg up. Let him put his foot down after a few seconds and praise him. If the horse struggles he must be held until he relaxes before he is allowed to put his foot down. If he is released while he is tense, a bigger struggle will result in the next session. The time his leg is held up

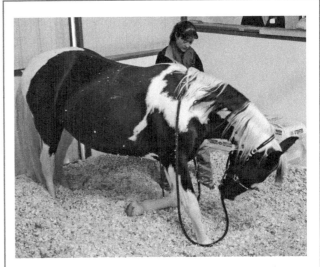

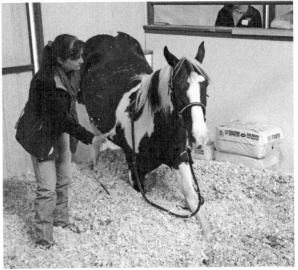

Bow in the "Lie Down Stall" deeply bedded with shavings.

may be increased incrementally. A few seconds increase per session is reasonable for most horses.

4. As the horse learns to lift his leg on cue and will hold it up as you support it with the slide rope, offer a treat in a way to encourage the horse to drop his body low to reach for it—just as in the Obeisance.

   The cannon bone should lower until it is parallel to the ground. Lure the horse with the treat to stretch down, rock back (slightly) and reach back with his head.

   In making this combination of moves, he will drop his body slightly and it may come as a complete surprise to him the first time his knee touches the ground. If so, reassure him and immediately offer a food reward. Continue practicing to the point that he automatically drops to his knee in the Bow with minimal support of the rigging.

5. When he is adept at lowering onto his bent leg in a bow, a whip cue can be introduced by tapping lightly on the front of the cannon bone with the handle. A light repetitive tapping with the intention of offering support usually works best.

6. Give the horse plenty of time to learn how to lower his body and gain strength and balance. He could get desperate to snatch a treat or regain his balance and could lunge forward or fall sideways. Support him as he masters this balancing act.

Generalize the Bow to new areas with the rigging for association.

The Trick Horse Companion

Horses may quickly understand the move yet not be able to comply for quite some time. This is one more reason we use the rigging—to give him confidence as he gains condition.

Adding a Bridle

As the horse learns to balance and drop to his knee while on three legs, a bridle can be added to help him draw his body back and slightly down. Rig him with a full cheek French link snaffle bit and headstall with reins attached. Stand on the horse's left side facing

Lift the leg and help the horse to rock his weight back a few inches. Use the lead to help him understand to shift his weight to the hind quarters.

The horse may be surprised the first time his knee actually touches the ground. Ask him to hold the position only a few seconds at first and tell him "Good" and praise him.

With a snaffle bit, use reins to slightly tip his nose over the supporting (right) leg. If he tries to lurch up, this position will encourage him to remain in position.

to the front of his body with the butt end of a short whip in your left hand along with the rigging rope. Put the reins in your right hand positioned at the center of the horse's top line, and just in front of the withers. A loop rein may be easier to handle than split reins.

It may take some practice to handle all the equipment but it will help the horse greatly with balance. The reins will block any forward movement and help you draw his body back and slightly down. Draw him back slowly and incrementally or the horse will lose his balance and become discouraged or resistant. If

he seems to be struggling with his balance, tip his nose slightly to the right, as this will place more of his weight on the outstretched, supporting right leg.

If using food rewards, treat for position, even if just an inch or so progress from the last repetition or last session. When releasing the horse after each repetition, let him move a few steps forward or walk around the stall to prevent claustrophobia.

Repeat the repetitions over multiple sessions, until he lifts his leg at the slightest tap

Mystic River learning to bow while mounted.

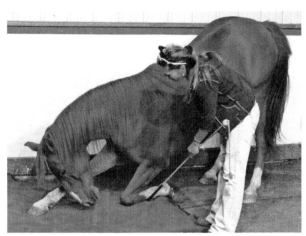

Kate Austin asks Navegador for a Bow. The rug protects his knee and can be used as a target.

and becomes lighter as he rocks his body back. As you cue the horse to lower his body, lower your upper body (head and shoulders) a bit so the horse can follow your movement as a cue.

It may take many repetitions over many days for the horse to achieve a real Bow. As he gains balance and confidence, ask him to "Whoa" while in position for longer yet reasonable periods of time before you release him. A release cue is always necessary.

When he executes the Bow easily and willingly, the reins can be used to encourage him to hold until given a Release Cue. The Bow is not complete, however until it can be done with the handler standing some distance from the horse and also when the horse is at liberty.

Teaching the Bow on the right side usually goes faster than the first, as the horse already understands the concept and has built his confidence and trust.

We may do three short sessions per day with no more than three or four repetitions each time.

Common Problems

- Walking out of position or wiggling around instead of yielding

- Can take a horse a long time and require much patience to learn

Tips

- Protect the knees of your horse. No move or trick is ever worth risking damage to a horse's body or joints. If he bruises a knee, he will begin to resist strongly and who could blame him?

- Practice the Bow using leg protection or in the Lie Down stall

- Associate the Bow with feeding time

- Introduce a whip cue only after the horse understands the physical move

- Introduce stretching for the Bow gradually as the horse gains condition

- Use a large piece of folded (double thick or more) carpet as a target and as a pad for the knee

For further information, see our DVD *"Fundamentals I".*

The Kneel

The Kneel comes naturally to all horses as they do it in the everyday process of lying down. Kneeling is easy for a horse to do on his own but it is a different matter to get the move on cue.

Teach the Kneel slowly and incrementally to help the horse develop trust, range of motion, strength and the mental conditioning required. The Kneel places him in an instinctually vulnerable position so keep his stress level low. The horse should be hobble trained so picking up and holding his leg(s) doesn't come as a surprise.

There is more than one technique to achieve the Kneel. Which one to choose depends on the prior education of the horse. If he has been taught to bow on each side before learning to kneel you may want to choose the Wall Method below. It is always good practice to teach the Kneel from each side of the horse.

Equipment

- Gloves

- Hobbles

- Rope—small diameter with a small snap on one end

- Polo wraps, three for each front leg, or shipping boots

- Halter and lead rope

- Feed in a small bucket

Goals

- Develop a slow, controlled and precise Kneel

- To isolate the Kneel from other related movements

- Prepare the horse for the Lie Down and Sit Up

Benefits

- The horse will develop an attitude of willing obedience and trust
  .
- Learning the incremental steps of the Kneel will help prepare the horse to go on to learn the Lie Down

Cues

- **Verbal cue** is "Kneel"

- **Proximity cue** is usually next to the horse's left shoulder and lowering your body slightly to mirror the move requested from the horse.

- **Physical cue** is to touch the horse's front cannon bone with the butt of a guider whip.

Steps

1. Wrap each front leg with two or three polo wraps layered and in a crisscross pattern, from mid-cannon bone to a few inches above the knee or padded shipping boots that cover the knee. Duct tape can be used to hold the shipping boots if needed. Place the surcingle and hobbles on the horse and rig the pull rope in the Running W arrangement.

2. Use the prepared Lie Down stall and

Even if a horse is properly prepared by having learned to bow on each side, he may be surprised the first time he is asked to kneel and both knees touch the ground.

position the horse in the middle. Calm, trustworthy horses may be schooled in a stall and those who are not should only be schooled in the outdoors Lie Down area. Weanlings and yearlings can usually be safely handled in a stall but an inexperienced handler may not be ready to make the quick decisions needed to remain in control and safe with a full sized horse.

One of the reasons we use the Running W rigging is if a horse should struggle, putting you or himself in danger, the rigging can instantly be released.

3. Stand on the left side of the horse with the lead rope and whip (yes, both) in your left hand and the pull rope in your right hand. An assistant can be a tremendous help to manage the lead rope(s). We use a regular lead for the primary handler and an additional lead to the right or off side for the assistant. The assistant can help keep a horse from spinning or getting stuck in a corner–for his and the handlers' safety.

4. Tap the horse's left (near) leg with the butt end of the whip and ask him to lift it. As he lifts his leg, support it by taking the slack out of the surcingle rope and hold it for a second or two. Release the leg and let him relax for a minute and praise him. Horses can get claustrophobic when a leg is taken away the first few times; be patient yet gently persistent.

5. Repeat the above steps until the horse is comfortable with the leg being taken away and understands you can be trusted to give it back in a reasonable length of time. This procedure may be spread over several days, as the time frame depends on the temperament and acceptance level of the horse. Teach the leg lift from both sides before proceeding to the Kneel.

It is normal for a horse to lie down after kneeling; however, we must be careful to isolate the Kneel from the Lie Down.

A nice Kneel is the first half of the Lie Down.

6. The next step is to ask for both legs almost simultaneously. Some horses resist giving or lifting the second leg. It may be necessary to rock the horse to one side or turn him to the side with the lead rope (and assistant) to put him slightly off balance so he takes a hop. As he takes the second foot off the ground or takes a hop, take the slack out of the pull rope. The rope and legs should be taken up quickly and smoothly without tightening your arm muscles. Tension can radiate down the rope and transfer to the horse. It requires practice and forethought to take the slack out of the rope. Any bobble in the handler's confidence may unnerve the horse and cause him to resist yielding his legs.

We usually cue the leg slightly above the fetlock followed by the same cue to the right fetlock. Both legs must be "caught" by the rope for a horse to kneel without hesitation or time to decide to struggle. If one leg is only slightly bent, you may want to release him and try another repetition. Do not be surprised or alarmed if the horse struggles, or if he doesn't. It is helpful to not hold preconceived notions about what may happen. A struggle is usually momentary and won't be a big deal unless we make a fuss about it.

7. Treating for position while he is on his knees helps take away fearful emotional responses and helps him to relax. Eating from the bucket while on his knees will

The Trick Horse Companion

reinforce his acceptance and confidence. Give a Bridge Signal of "Good" and immediately put a small bucket of feed under his nose. If you feel he will stay on his knees for a few seconds, let him eat. If you sense that he will hop up, let him.

We have had student horses literally eat while in the Kneel position for a week or more. The more time a horse spends on his knees (within reason) eating, the more comfortable he will become as eating diffuses tension. Feed in the small bucket can gradually be replaced with a few food treats.

Do not expect the horse to gracefully lower himself to the ground for some time. As he becomes comfortable kneeling, his balance will improve along with his confidence. Many horses will go ahead and lie down on their own while on their knees. We may choose to allow this while still teaching the Kneel and later on after the Lie Down has been learned, go back and separate the Kneel from the Lie Down.

The Kneel may be taught in the Lie Down stall or outdoors on the Lie Down area. Tipping the head slightly to one side encourages the horse not to lurch up.

Give lots of dwell time between sessions either by tying him in a quiet place or hand walking him.

If you have prepared your horse thoroughly up to this point, he should be confident and trusting even while on his knees.

Wall Method

If a horse has been taught the Bow prior to learning the Kneel, this method is fine. Wrap his knees and position him parallel and next to the wall in the Lie Down stall. Positioning him against the wall is for his physical support and to prevent him from evading. Stand on his right side and ask him to Bow with his left leg. While he is in the Bow position, ask him to hold or stay as you tap him on the cannon bone or ankle of the right leg with the butt end of the whip.

Often a horse will draw one leg back and then the other to drop to both knees. If he does this, reward him quickly and release him. If the horse resists this method, it would be best to move to the standard method as above.

Common Problems
Wiggling and walking out of position
Do not lose your composure or confidence if the horse struggles. Remain calm, stay cool and start again. Small skirmishes are no big deal and should not deter you.

A variation of the Kneel is this position called a "Chest Let Down." The carpet keeps the colt's confidence in executing the move because it protects his knees.

Tips

- Horses are very protective of their knees, so use adequate leg protection

- Ask only for a very brief Kneel at first; a second or two touchdown with both knees is enough

- Keep sessions short—two or three repetitions per session

- The type of whip touch or cue to the horse's legs depends on his sensitivity to your encouraging/guiding touch

- A piece of carpet can be used as a target or spot for the horse to kneel

- Horses can become claustrophobic when a leg is taken away. Teach your horse you can be trusted to always give the leg back

- Do not ask a horse to kneel on the trail or any hard surface that could bruise or scrape his legs. Doing so will reduce the likelihood he will ever be willing to kneel for you again

- As the horse becomes proficient at giving the Kneel, rigging can be reduced and the handler may increase his distance from the horse.

- Do not ask for a Kneel on grass. Horses will cheat by trying to eat and will not be able to concentrate

The Lie Down

A Modern Perspective

There are lots of tricks to teach a horse for fun and for reasons of increasing his intelligence and cooperation. The Lie Down, however, is a move we believe is for the benefit and safety of the horse. When properly taught, the Lie Down gives a horse the confidence and courage to stay down, where he is at and in almost any situation, until he is released. The release may come from the handler as a cue telling him to rise or even to go into a Sit Up. It may also come as the release from some dangerous entanglement situation such as a trailer wreck, being cast against a wall, caught in a fence or even trapped in a

Photo: Paula da Silva

cattle guard. The Lie Down teaches the horse that his handler is in total control of the situation and he can depend on him for help if he is in trouble.

Mary Stewart and Lady C pose for a photo shoot with Penny Stone.

Laying horses down is quite popular in equine expos, clinics and competitions especially those devoted to taming horses. While laying horses down can be beneficial, the method and manner in which this happens can vary greatly. At Imagine a Horse, the Lie Down is used for entirely different reasons and goals than to tame a horse or to offer remedial solutions to undesirable behaviors.

Lying down is a natural process that comes with the animal by virtue of physical ability and instinctive behavior horses can choose to do. Laying a horse down often brings a handler face to face with a horse's inherent fight-or-flight behavior.

We teach the Lie Down as a multistep process, taught incrementally with great attention to detail especially in providing safety and comfort to the horse. In learning the Lie Down, he will have learned how to Kneel, Lie Down, Lay Down Flat, Roll Up, extend each front leg separately and even retract them, all on cue. Our method helps the horse duplicate the exact series of steps (on cue) he makes when he lies down of his own accord. Horses go down first to the knee (carpus), assume a sternal position, lower the hip and finally go recumbent, often rolling laterally onto the side.

The horse is active in the process as it is taught to him incrementally and he is rewarded for each step of his progress.

Most (other) methods to lay a horse down involve some variation of tying a horse's leg up and putting him off balance by pulling his head around or by picking up a front leg and rocking him back from a bow-like position until he goes down. Having the leg of a horse tied up or bound with a knee hobble seems a rather risky method for creating the Ultimate Companion Horse. Tired muscles are most prone to injury. Another problem with tying

a leg up is there is no quick release for the horse if he panics or gets in trouble.

Picking a horse's leg up with your hand and rocking him back can cause him to roll on his shoulder to lie down toward the handler, a move that is dangerous and awkward. Because this is not the natural way in which horses lie down, most will eventually come to resent rolling on the shoulder.

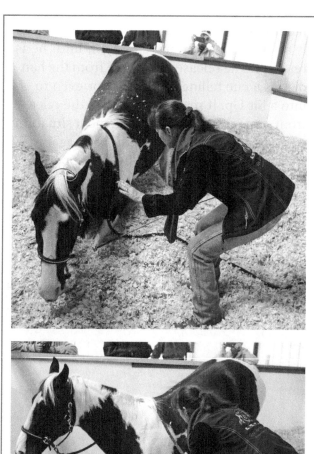

Sue's body position helps Lady C understand what she is asking.

Sombra knelt quietly and obediently and began to fold her hind legs to lie down.

She temporarily got stuck and Allen helped her by putting slight pressure on the bridle to tell her to continue down.

This is most often seen with handlers not having sufficient experience to actually understand the process of laying a horse down.

Also popular today are "no rope" methods. While the idea is very nice to think of, the reality is it will take most horses a very long time to learn to lie down on cue without at least some type of support to help them balance.

The Imagine A Horse method is facilitated with Lie Down rigging and is a no-nonsense method. At the same time, we believe it to be the safest and most humane method for the horse. There are many nuances of developing willing obedience a horse will learn along the way. For instance, he will learn in no uncertain terms that "Whoa" or to lie still until given another cue means exactly that. He will learn to stay on a "mark," to lie down, not wiggle and offer evasions. He will learn to accept a physical AND mental attitude of self-restraint and trust, which leads to com-

With a little bit pressure, Allen urged her to stay in position and not lurch up.

Sombra willingly extended each front leg as Allen cued her to "Come Out."

pliance.

Some horses learn the entire process of the Lie Down in a few days, and we have had others that learned it over a course of weeks. The confidence the horse has in us is sacred; it is far too important for us to get in a hurry and throw him or push him beyond his physical and mental capabilities.

We want him to completely realize we have put him in this position, that he is in no danger and we can be trusted to release him. In teaching a horse restraint of any kind including hobble use, it is the handler who is earning the horse's trust, not the horse earning the handler's trust! Compliance follows trust.

In teaching the Lie Down, a handler must make instant decisions, especially in an indoor area. It is always wise to observe an experienced trainer and to work with only those horsemen and women you trust completely both personally and with your horse.

Equipment

- Gloves

- Leather surcingle with padded bellyband and three D-rings sewn and riveted in

- Hobbles

- Rope—small diameter with a small snap on one end

- Polo wraps, two for each front leg

- Padded shipping boots

- Halter and two long lead ropes

Goals

- The horse will Lie Down at Liberty on cue, roll upright while still down, extend and withdraw front legs and rise in a controlled and obedient manner

- Complete and willing trust and submission by the horse

Benefits

The Lie Down has a huge carry-over effect in all facets of a horse's personality. The horse usually comes to a position of complete trust and willing obedience.

Cues

- **Verbal cue** is "Lie Down"

Another quiet Lie Down sequence with Sombra yielding to bit pressure.

As Boullet begins to lie down, Allen tips his nose slightly to the off (right) side to urge him to lie with his back towards him.

Allowing a horse to observe his surroundings from his new position helps him to relax and stay alert.

This is the safest way to reach across the horse and unclip the slip rope.

- **Proximity cue** is usually at the left side of the horse, facing the horse and slightly in front of his shoulder. Lower your body as you cue him to lower his.

- **Physical cue** is a tap on the cannon bone (as in the Kneel and Bow) to ask him to kneel. While in the kneeling position we use a gentle tapping on the gaskin with a guider whip to soften and relax the hind leg muscles.

Steps

Refer to the initial preparation as described in the Kneel. Most horses will lie down on their own in the final stages of learning the Kneel, which usually signifies the horse is totally relaxed with the process. If he has become accustomed to doing this, it will be much easier for him to get to the Lie Down on cue. It is usually worth a little more time spent in the Kneel process to make the Lie Down easier on both you and the horse.

The horse must lie down when and where he is cued and in the proper order, which is to assume the Kneel and then lower the hind end down slowly. We absolutely do not want the horse to just flop over on his side!

Position the horse in the middle of a level mound of shavings or slightly used bedding mixed with straw in the outdoor Lie Down area. Ask for the Kneel and wait for him to lie down as you tap gently on his gaskin with the guider whip. If he has been adequately prepared in learning the Kneel, this is generally an easy and non-traumatic transition. If he gets locked in the Kneel position, use the halter rope to tip his head slightly around to the off side. This should create a slight bend through his body, which will set him up to properly lie down with his back toward you.

It is normal for a horse to occasionally get stuck in position. Stroking him on the gaskin with a guider whip usually relaxes him and helps him to continue down.

Tipping his head to his right or off side makes it difficult for him to hop up because he cannot leverage his body up without full use of his neck. During initial training, we always want the horse to lie with his back toward us and never with his feet toward us. We may teach the Lie Down from both sides but we usually want him to lie with his back toward us. Occasionally, if one just can't easily learn to lie on a particular side, it is not worth the trauma to force him to lie unnaturally.

Be prepared to wait the horse out if he becomes stuck in the Kneel, and do not attempt to force him down. Be patient and wait quietly. If he puts up a struggle, stick with him unless you assess there is real danger of hurting himself. This means real danger, not necessarily a struggle.

Helping a horse to lie flat then roll him upright into the "Sphinx" position is as mentally beneficial as repetitions of lying down but without the physical exertion.

You must be prepared mentally how to best handle each horse's struggles. In any event, your calm and kind attitude will definitely influence the horse.

Three or four repetitions of lying down are usually a horse's mental limit per session.

It is common for a horse's muscles, especially the shoulders, to quiver, sometimes very noticeably. This is most likely an adrenaline response that occurs because the horse's ability to flee has been taken away. We generally stroke or rub the shaking muscles and walk the horse forward around the lie down area once he is back on his feet. The shaking will resolve as the horse understands he is safe.

Many horses lie down quite willingly the

first couple of days and then experience a post-learning dip and decide "not today," which is quite natural. If the horse refuses, refrain from frustration and do not attempt to force him down. You may want to tie him in a quiet place so he can have a little time out before trying again. Your patience will be most helpful to his understanding.

When the horse lies down easily, decrease the equipment required by going to just a Running V, and decrease the number of polo wraps. Many horses will associate both the training location and the rigging with the act of lying down. At this stage, the handler may

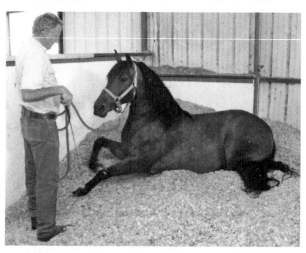

If a horse is to continue to the Sit Up and Sit Down it is important that he learn to extend each front leg separately on cue as he remains in the Sphinx position.

still rig the horse for this reason, yet choose not to use the ropes.

The horse may be taught to lie down on the left side only or from either side. The preference is the handler's decision.

Roll Up and Lie Flat

A horse could easily develop a sense of learned helplessness if he were to be laid down repeatedly in a short time span. Old timers often referred to this as "breaking the horse's spirit." We definitely do not want to do this. Learned helplessness happens when people or animals become conditioned to believe a situation is hopeless and there is no escape, so they give up.

To prevent the learned helplessness syndrome and still achieve the same profound

It is a great idea to have a trained horse lie down quietly so the student can watch. Here Kristi reassures Cal that he "can do it." It is the assistant's job to keep the horse straight and out of the main handler's space

Even a properly prepared horse can panic and take a leap. Kristi and Allen both remained calm, soothed Cal and went back to work.

effects of multiple repetitions, we have found it effective to teach the horse to lie flat (sometimes called playing dead), to roll to the upright position and then lie back down flat.

Rolling Up from the flat position and then down seems to have the same effects on the horse without the full effort required to lie down repeatedly from a standing position. We may allow a horse to roll into an upright position and then ask him to lie flat five or six times per session. This does not seem to bother most horses at all.

We make it a habit to deeply massage a horse's neck while he is lying flat as this is one of the very few times it is not supporting his rather heavy head! Most of them seem to really enjoy the massage. Caution: Don't put your face near or above the horse's head when he is lying flat. If he lurches, you could receive a hard knock.

Have an assistant walk all around a horse while he is lying flat so he becomes accustomed to seeing a human above him from all angles. It is fine to sit on the hip of a horse while he is lying down but not on his ribs or belly. Asking for a Smile also helps to relax a horse while he is down.

We urge you not to stand on your horse as this appears to diminish his stature.

Many horses readily lie flat and others resist strongly. If your horse resists, we must create a situation in which he feels safe and confident in relinquishing his power to escape at will. This may be done with stroking, offering food in a bucket, a food treat or backing up a few steps in the training.

A steep mound of shavings can be shaped so when he is lying down, he will be able to move slightly off center (from his body) with his head to rest it against the shavings. This

may seem awkward if you have only taught him to lie down with his back toward you. We sometimes use the small end of a teardrop-shaped Bean Bag like a pillow for him to rest his head on. When a horse has learned he is safe and is also made comfortable by laying his head on the beanbag or mound, the time spent lying flat can be slowly increased.

We often ask a horse to Smile while he is lying down. When a horse smiles, it seems to take his mind off his current situation and focus on something different and pleasant.

Get Up or Release

He must learn to remain down, either with his legs tucked in and under in the Sphinx position, with legs extended or flat out until he is released to get up. We always want the horse to rise with his front end first rather than with his hind end.

While the horse is lying flat out, carefully reach across his shoulder or girth area and unclip the snap on the right side of the rigging rope. If possible, shake the rope a little to loosen it so he can rise up (on cue) without struggling to get his feet free. If the tension is not released on the rope, it may result in his getting up hind end first, which we must prevent because it is almost impossible to go back and correct later. If he raises his hind end first, he can't learn to Sit Up.

Tell him to "Get Up" and tap him on the shoulder (either side) to urge him to raise his front end up normally.

Extending and Retracting the Front Legs on Cue

Extending the front legs individually while in the Lie Down will help to condition the horse to raise his front end first. It also requires thoughtful obedience and teaches him to accept restraint on an entirely new level. He has already learned that escape is not an option with the handler in complete control of his actions.

Seriously, just imagine the level of compliance and concentration it requires for him to remain lying and extend or retract each leg on request!

While some folks will absolutely not see the benefit of this portion of the Lie Down, it is required of all of our horses.

Prepare a large bank or mound of shavings large enough for the horse to lie on to extend

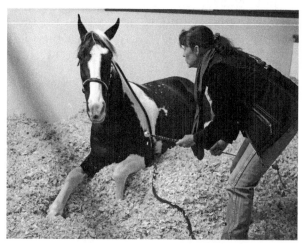

Lady C extended each front leg as Sue asked and also retracted them on cue.

his legs off the side of the mound when assuming the Sphinx (sternal recumbent) position. This position seems to make most horses more comfortable and allows him to easily extend each leg as cued.

While the horse is lying down in the upright position with his back toward you and legs folded under his body, tap his right (off) shoulder with a guider whip and tell him to "come out." If he has been conditioned (and cued) to lie down from his left side, he will need to extend his right leg as it will be almost impossible to get his left out from under his body first. He will also need his right leg to extend first in support of his neck and head, which will be tipped slightly over the right leg. Teach the extension on one leg at a time.

Extending each leg on cue may take a considerable investment of time and energy and is a finishing touch of precision and total compliance. The hard work has already been done in teaching (up to this point) the entire realm of Tricks of Trust. There are lots of folks who lay horses down but virtually no one else teaches this!

Common Problems

- Wiggling or walking out of the position (place) where he is asked to lie down

- Can't extend a front leg if it is stuck under his body

- Crowding or pushing into the handler

- Spinning the hindquarters around or dragging his body backwards while in the Kneel position

- Lurching up

- Rising with the hind end first
- Trying to roll is not encouraged while he is lying down

Tips

- If an assistant is involved, take the time to "brief" him or her prior to the process.

- Stay out of range of the horse's front feet and to the side so he cannot lunge forward into you if he tries to get up. An assistant holding a second lead rope while standing on the opposite side of the horse (never in front) is a very good idea.

- A tense or worried assistant will prove more of a hindrance than a help as the horse will sense insecurity and reflect it in his behavior.

- Stay relaxed and soft regardless of the situation the horse is presenting. Any tension in your body will be transmitted down the ropes like a message on a telegraph line.

- The shape of the bedding mound can be used advantageously to lay the horse down so his back is uphill and the legs are downhill. This position gives the greatest comfort and ease of rising (something not lost on a horse).

- When a horse is Kneeling and his back legs are straight or stuck in a standing position, tap rhythmically or stroke his gaskin to help him relax and fold his back legs into the Lie Down.

- It's beneficial to roll the horse to an upright position or dog position from lying flat and then back down flat.
- If a horse tries to roll when he lies down, tap him with the guider whip and tell him "No."

- During the entire process, the less you move your feet, the better. If the horse perceives he can make you move, he is in control. Staying in your own tracks sends a message of confidence and control.

For further information, see our DVD *"Fundamentals II".*

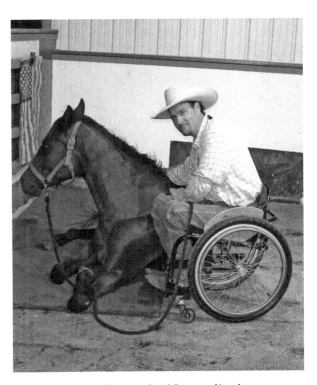

Michael Richardson asked Dos to lie down on the carpet.

The Sit Up

While the Sit Up and Sit Down may look like the same position, they are each achieved through a completely different process. The Sit Up is taught from the lie down/Sphinx position while the Sit Down is executed from the standing position. In other words, the achieved position is almost the same but the mechanics are very different for each and they are two separate tricks. This means they must be taught separately. Horses usually figure out at some point the end position is the same, but it may take a long time.

Proper preparation of the training area for either the Sit Up or Sit Down escalates learning. We prepare the stall area with lots of big flake shavings just as we did in teaching the Kneel and Lie Down.

We never sit a horse up while he is on the ground as he can easily bruise or otherwise injure his hocks. Thick turf is okay for a dem-

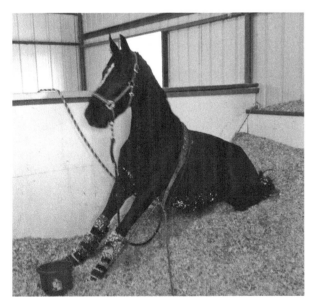

Good preparation of the training area makes the Sit Up easy for the horse to understand.

onstration or single repetition. As in teaching all Tricks of Trust, preparation and protection of the horse is very important. The safety and comfort of our horse is never too much trouble!

Equipment

- Gloves

- Halter and lead rope

- Bridle with full cheek French link snaffle and reins

- Surcingle

Benefits

- Strengthens the front end and back of the horse

- Increased body balance and mental control

- Lessons in self-control carry over to other activities

Cues

- **Verbal cue** is "Sit UP"

- **Proximity cue** is next to the horse's left shoulder and slightly in front of his body, facing his back end

- **Physical cue** can be a light tap on the left shoulder after he has learned to sit up

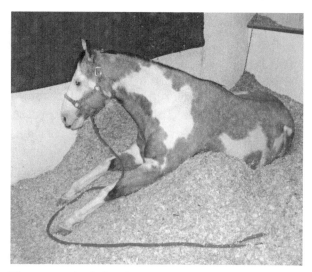

The mound of shavings supports the horse and puts him in a partial sitting position when he extends his front legs from the Lie Down.

Steps

1. Halter the horse and clip the lead rope to the cheek ring on the right side instead of under the chin. This allows you to lift the head without twisting it.

   The shavings will be piled high in the corner into a bank that is similar in shape to the teardrop-shaped beanbag with the narrow end pointing upward. The shavings as they taper down should still be packed at the base to provide firm footing. This is where the horse will kneel. Beyond the kneel area, the bank of shavings will drop off a little so that when the horse lies down and is cued to bring both front legs out in front of him, they will extend over the bank, his belly will be supported by the mound of shavings and he will be in a partial sitting position. The comfort and support of his body will expedite the learning of this move dramatically.

2. It is a good idea to ask for many partial rises and also drops (lowering) from the Lie Down. This builds strength and body control and is easier on the horse than repetitions of lying down and then assuming the sit position.

3. Cue the horse to lie down in an upright position. From the upright position ask him to extend both front legs, one at a time while remaining down. His breastbone area or sternum should be directly

From an upright lie down position, the horse extends both front legs and raises his body slightly.

The complete Sit Up progression.

1

2

Boullet receives his reward.

4

5

Boullet stays nicely in position.

Charisma kneels and continues to lie down quietly

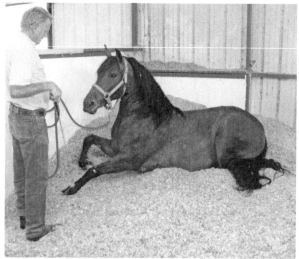

Charisma stayed in position until Allen cued her to extend her front legs.

on the edge of the supporting bank of shavings while his extended legs will be on the downhill side of the bank. This will result in a partial sitting position. Some horses rise into the sit with only a "Whoa" cue and others will (try to) lurch up. Treating for position usually works well, especially from a bucket.

If the horse lurches up and does not get the concept of rising slowly into the Sit Up or refuses to try, proceed to using the bridle and snaffle bit.

Attach reins to a full cheek snaffle and cross them at a position over the horse's withers as was done in teaching the Bow.

Repeat the Lie Down and cue for the legs to be extended. You will stand next to the horse's withers facing his head, the reins will be in your right hand, the lead and whip in your left hand. Ask the horse to rise slightly by tapping him on the left shoulder. Take up slight contact with the reins to steady him and keep him in place. Catch him with a firmer hold if he tries to lurch or rise more than a couple of inches. Make the right rein a little shorter so his nose is tipped slightly to the right. A horse cannot lurch up without full use of his neck for strength and balance.

Rising into a Sit takes a lot of strength and can be exhausting mentally and physically.

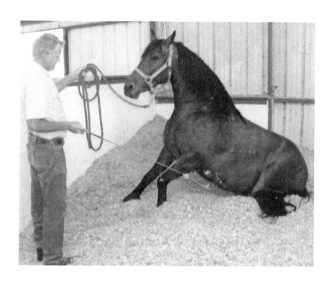

The Trick Horse Companion

Prevent Lurching, Control the Head

Tack the horse with a bridle, blanket and surcingle. On some horses the blanket helps keep the surcingle in place, on others it will cause it to slip. A light rope of about 12 to 15 feet with a snap on one end will be needed.

Snap the rope to the highest ring of the surcingle on the off (right) side of the horse. Bring the other end through the bit ring and back through the high surcingle ring. The remainder of the rope will cross over the top of the horse's back to be held in your right hand. This will create a draw rein on the right side of the horse's rigging.

Acquaint the horse with the draw rein arrangement by slightly applying pressure and asking him to yield his nose to the right. Do not twist his head around; instead, ask him to yield lightly.

Be soft with your feel to let him know even though you are in control of his head, he has nothing to fear. The draw rein is constricting, and if the horse feels claustrophobic he may learn to resist strongly no matter how much pressure is put on the rein. Tact is a must to maintain his trust, while preventing him from lurching up rather than sitting up slowly.

Have the horse lie down on the mound of

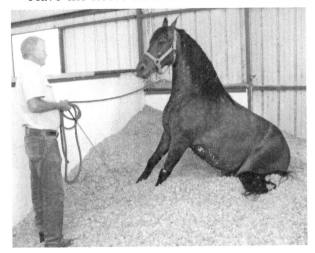

Charisma's sit up position is perfect.

shavings and extend his front feet. Ask him to walk his front feet back toward his chest with baby steps as he lifts his body. He must support his weight as he takes these tiny steps and at the same time rise ever so slightly. As he is doing this, very gently tip his head to the right and hold it there for a few seconds before allowing him to sink back down. Sinking back down to the lying position will be a familiar release of pressure for him.

A few repetitions will usually convince the horse there is no need to struggle. If he continues to lurch up or struggle, he may not be able (yet) to control his body sufficiently to rise up. Some horses don't have the strength to push their bodies up. If you determine that he doesn't, you can always come back to this lesson in a month or two.

If a horse struggles for no apparent reason, you will have virtually no option than to quickly squelch his attempts by putting him back down. Most horses realize quickly that rising into the Sit Up is much easier than jumping up only to be immediately cued to lie back down.

Common Problems

- Lurching up rather than trying to sit up

- The horse's front feet slip forward and he cannot get traction to raise his front end up

Tips

- The Sit Up requires a lot of strength to learn.

- Keep your feet well to the side of the horse so he can't stomp on them if he lurches up.

- Screw cleats or runner boards into the floor for the horse to brace his feet on.

- Floor cleats need to be small—about 1.25 inches square and at least two feet long. Place them perpendicular to the wall, about 10 inches apart. We make them by ripping a common 2x4 in half lengthwise and rounding the corners. Screw them securely to the floor through the rubber mats.

- The higher the bank of shavings under the horse's breast and belly, the easier it will be for him to Sit Up.

- When making a mound for the Sit Up, pack the shavings down to make it supportive.

- The mound must be constantly re-shaped between repetitions.

- A dedicated lie down pile outdoors made of old hay and shavings keeps its shape better if the edges are packed down and mixed with a little clean soil.

The Sit Down

In preparation to learn the Sit Down, a horse must be capable of Tricks of Trust taught to this point as most just can't be taught from a standing position. Occasionally a very compliant adolescent horse can be taught to sit from a standing position but this usually is not the case.

We will link the Lie Down and Kneel with a simultaneous crouching action of the hind end. As the horse kneels, we cue him to drop his hindquarters, simultaneously flip out his front legs and lift his front end. This series of moves results in a teeter-totter type mo-tion. As you may imagine, the Tricks of Trust must be confirmed and the horse must be obedient, willing and easily controlled. Most horses eagerly sit down when they realize it is easier than going through the entire teeter-totter type sequence.

We have seen trainers whip the hind legs of the horse until he takes a fearful crouching position. This is usually done to make a horse sit all the way down on flat ground. We feel sitting down into the dirt is something no horse would ever do on his own. We never do this because of the risk to the horse's legs.

Teaching a trick through fear or intimidation is never a good idea. When a horse has been whipped into submission, it shows in his demeanor and how he quickly drops to the ground with disregard for his own comfort.

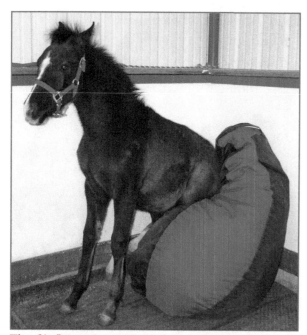

The Sit Down is most easily taught to a foal or young horse.

This is a very difficult trick. Our method is respectful to his long-term wellbeing and most of all, his sentience.

The Sit Down will give your horse a completely new way of using his body. He must learn to use his muscles, balance and coordination in ways he would never attempt on his own. Be patient and forgiving. Two or three successful approximations are all we should ask in one session.

Give the horse adequate time between sessions to assimilate this process. Several short sessions throughout the day with with "dwell time" in between to integrate the new learning is what we suggest.

Ask your horse to Sit Down first thing in the morning and instead of a treat give a small bucket of his favorite food. This creates a powerful and positive incentive to learn and a reason to stay sitting.

Equipment

- Gloves

- Hobbles

- Leg protection for front legs

- Halter and lead rope

- Beanbag

- Small bucket of feed

- Long rope and eye ring screwed into one corner of the training stall

Cues

- **Vocal cue** is "Sit Down"

- **Proximity cue** is to stand on the left side of the horse, facing him

- **Physical cue** to step him back and lightly tap or softly stroke his gaskin

Steps

1. Prepare the Lie Down stall with large pile of shavings in the corner, as in the Sit Up. This will be the target for the horse to sit on and it needs to support his weight. The pile of shavings will need to be re-shaped often and is worth the effort.

   Shovel a large mound in the corner and walk it to pack it as you pile it up. Dig out the front face of the pile to create a "cliff" to back the horse into so his back legs make contact with it. This mound will give him confidence there is actually something behind to support him or lean against. Leave a layer of shavings in front of the pile so the horse can kneel with protection for his knees, which will also add to his confidence.

2. Position the horse parallel to the wall and back him into the corner of the stall and mound of shavings until his hind end touches it. He may lean against the wall for support. This is a trick in itself, and can be done several times with a walk around the stall in between to help him relax.

   If he has not learned to separate the Kneel from the Lie Down, go back and solidify that aspect before proceeding.

3. When the horse is comfortable with backing against the pile of shavings, cue him to kneel just in front of it. Keep his head raised slightly with a close hold on the lead of the halter Devote a session or two just asking him to kneel in front of the pile of shavings.

4. When you feel he is relaxed, ask him to kneel, and as he does, lift his head slightly to help prevent him from trying to lie down. At the same time, tap his gaskin and ask him to lower his hind end as he does when lying down. As he begins to lower his bottom, lift the head a little more, keeping his body upright. His body must stay straight and he can't be allowed to drop his nearside shoulder as he lowers.

   As he is lowering his rear end, lift the head more and tap the nearside front leg to ask him to extend his front legs. When this sequence is coordinated, the horse's body will move like a teeter-totter; as the back end is going down, the front end will be rising. This is a complex series and is unlike anything he has ever done. He could lose his balance or flail outward with his front legs. Stay calm and keep your feet out of his way.

   The surprise of completing this series of moves may translate into a lurch upward. Don't try to stop him but praise him lavishly for his effort, which will help keep him calm and his confidence level up.

   The horse may try a few evasions before he comes to understand what is being asked. An obedient horse will follow the cues even though he doesn't exactly know what to anticipate. Finding himself in the Sit Down position may come as a complete surprise to him. Have a small bucket of feed within reach to put immediately under his nose so he may eat while in position.

To prevent a horse from lurching up before being released when sitting, we use a large diameter, extra long and soft rope snapped into an eye-hook screw in the corner of the Lie Down stall. While the horse is sitting, bring the rope across the center of his chest and hold it in your right hand. Keep it snug but not tight across his chest and use it as a barrier if he wants to get up before released. This is also an effective and non-threatening way to teach foals to respect restraint of a rope with no chance of hurting them. The rope can be dropped quickly if needed.

Transition to the Beanbag

The pile of shavings should be used during the initial training stages of the Sit Down. When the horse is consistent with the Sit Down, you may begin the process of transitioning the horse to sit on a Beanbag, a carpet-covered bale of hay or any other safe seat.

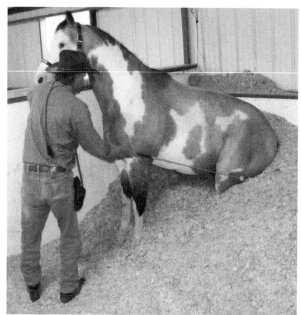

Shaping a big pile of shavings to support the horse in the sitting position is a big help and expedites completion of the move. The Bean Bag is buried in the pile and gradually emerges from the shavings.

The Sit Down initially combines elements of the Kneel, Lie Down and Come Out of the front legs in a type of teeter-totter move. While in the kneel position, the horse begins to drop his hindquarters and simultaneously extends both front legs as he raises his upper body.

The transition to the Beanbag is taught to the horse as a separate step or trick. Do not assume because he sits down on cue he will automatically sit on a different seat.

We prefer the Beanbag because it is light and easy to move around. The nature of its construction allows it to conform to the odd angles of a horse's rear end when sitting.

Because the Beanbag is a unique object, the horse can quickly associate the action with sitting with the Beanbag. Horses will not create a useful association with a bale of hay other than to eat it. Cover the bale with a quilted furniture moving pad or a piece of carpet and he will then make somewhat of an association.

Initially the sight, sound and crinkly feel of a new Beanbag is more than most horses can deal with. He likely will not want to be near it, or have it behind him, let alone touching his butt. This is understandable—it is only fair to expect to give him opportunities to see, smell and touch it as he chooses. We let student horses observe a trained horse sitting on a Beanbag and leave one in the training stall so they can get accustomed to seeing it. Move the bag from corner to corner so the horse can see it from all angles in close proximity.

Dig away the entire pile of shavings he was accustomed to sitting on. Place the Beanbag in the same corner, and cover it completely with shavings. The stall should look as though nothing has changed since training the Sit Up or Sit Down on the shavings pile.

Bring the horse to the stall and cue him to sit on the pile of shavings, hiding the Beanbag. The best scenario is he will be comfortable and sit down without hesitation. Over the course of a few sessions the Beanbag will

The cues for the Sit Down are gradually transferred from ground handler to rider.

The Trick Horse Companion

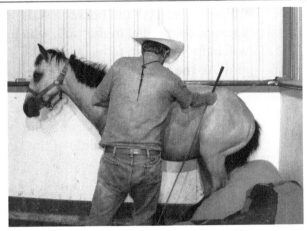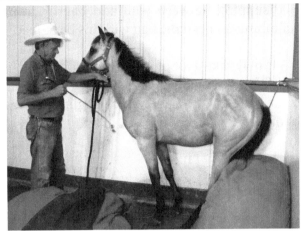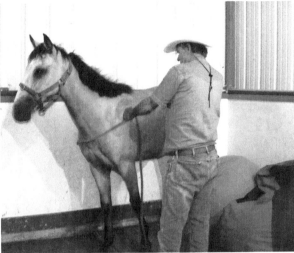

The Sit Down sometimes can be taught from a standing position if the horse is extremely compliant and yields easily. We use a chest rope to encourage the horse to move backwards and keep him from lurching up. Treat for position immediately with a bucket of feed.

slowly begin to emerge from under the shavings. If the horse remains calm and obedient about sitting there is no need to cover it again. If he is accepting, you may want to cover the Beanbag with a furniture pad or blanket to protect it.

Even though the horse may have learned to Sit Down, details to keeping it "crisp" in his mind are still needed. Do not allow him to walk backwards and climb onto the bag with his back feet and legs. This is usually a sign of nervousness or lack of understanding, and he

may need to go back a few steps in the process to the point that he is once again relaxed.

It is a HUGE leap of faith for a horse to lower his rear end down onto an object!

Prevent him from getting his hind leg between the bag and the wall. Sooner or later this will happen before he learns to solidly target the bag.

If he persists, use a hobble and rope on a hind leg and hold it forward to prevent the leg slipping between wall and bag or from climbing up onto the bag with his back feet.

It may take a lot of practice until the horse backs to the Beanbag and sits down with his rear end straight, offering no wiggling or evasions.

Sit Down Tips

- The horse should be acclimated to each new location that he is asked to sit down. This is called generalizing a trick.

- It is best to prop a beanbag up against a pedestal or wall if the horse will be asked to sit on it outside—this prevents it from slipping out from under him or rolling backwards.

- The Sit Down will have to be generalized, which is achieved by moving the beanbag to different locations. Initially use other corners of the

training stall. Ask the horse to walk backwards parallel to the wall, which will help him learn to back straight and use the beanbag as a target.

- Next step is to place the bag against the middle of the wall and start the horse backing in the middle of the stall. Help guide the horse by using a pair of whips, one on each side, to help line him up.

- It helps to have a second pedestal to create a false wall to help the horse line up to sit when practicing in a wide-open space.

For further information see our DVD *"Fundamentals II".*

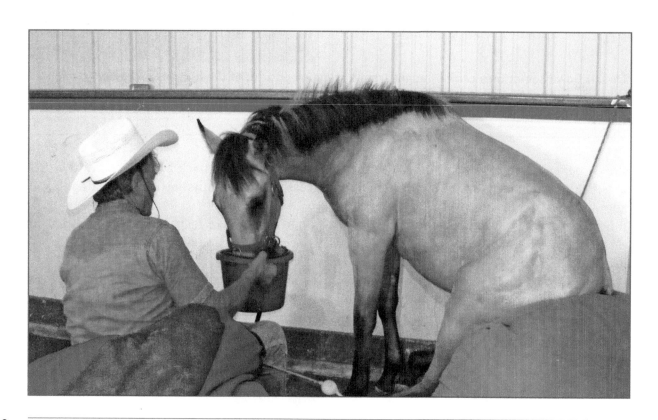

The Trick Horse Companion

The Rear

Getting High: Teaching the Rear Safely

The Rear is a beautiful and natural move for a horse. Rearing is done among horses playing and posturing for position in a herd, especially among stud colts and stallions. In posturing, the Rear is usually an attempt to keep his eye above the level of a challenging horse. Rearing makes a horse taller and more formidable as a challenger.

Lady C "Rockin the Stars and Stripes."

Pusher Rocks on the climbing wall.

The Trick Horse Companion

Rearing is an emotional expression.

Most trainers caution against teaching the Rear, as it can be dangerous if offered as an evasion, fun or a refusal to move forward.

Horses have traditionally been taught to rear while mounted, a dangerous practice as this is done with bit pressure and a horse can easily go over backwards. Other common methods include whipping or striking a horse's front legs, causing them to retract the legs and rear as a defensive move, resulting in an unbalanced position.

We teach the Rear on the ground in association with a pedestal. The horse has a clear target for his front feet as he moves and reaches forward in balance. Creating the association with the pedestal helps him shift his weight to the rear, unweight his front end and remain in balance. Stomping the feet down is a natural inclination and is how they attack an enemy critter. The mechanics of the stomping and of rearing are instinctual and seem to offer intrinsic reward.

Using a climbing wall gives the horse a target and helps him balance by putting his front feet on the horizontal rungs similar to how he used the cleat board. He squats on his hind end and spreads his back feet as he gains strength and agility for the standalone Rear. The climbing wall removes the emotion from rearing and gives him time to get accustomed to standing tall.

Some horses have the level head required to rear under saddle, which is a separate trick and process.

Very Important
The Rear is a beautiful, gymnastic move. To intimidate or hurt a horse to achieve quick compliance will not result in a beautiful Rear with poise and balance.

The climbing wall helps a horse learn balance and boldness and how to get his weight onto his hindquarters.

Equipment

- Halter and lead rope

- Pedestal

Cues

- **Vocal cue** can be "Hup" or simply "Up"

- **Proximity cue** is in front of the horse and on the opposite side of the pedestal, on the left side of the horse, facing him

- **Physical cue** can be the flick of a schooling whip at his shoulder or behind him to encourage forward movement

Common Problems

- Rearing without being asked or when asked for other moves

Rearing Tips

- Remember the horse must develop the strength for the Rear in his hindquarters, loins and hocks. This will not happen without proper conditioning.

- Yes, a horse can rear anytime, but training to achieve a balanced rear on cue is much safer.

- The only method that works when a horse rears inappropriately under saddle is to drive him forward.

Half Rear From a Halt

Ask the horse to "Step Up" on the pedestal with his front feet. As his leading leg lifts, swish the schooling whip on the backside of the cannon bone of the following leg, still on the ground or just beginning to lift. Encourage him to quickly pick it up. A swish of the whip behind the rump may be a better motivational move for some horses.

Use the lead rope with your left hand, to give short bumps on his nose if he tries to come over the pedestal. In following repetitions make increased speed the goal and raise your own energy level to help him understand he needs to hustle, which will make it easier to lift his front feet off the ground together. Praise even small lifts at this point. If he is a well-mannered horse, he may have a difficult time rearing as it may be out of his emotional comfort zone.

When your horse understands hustling to the pedestal, concentrate on creating more momentum and a higher lift.

Half Rear, Longeing to the Pedestal

Put the horse on a 12- to 15-foot working line and longe him in circles around the pedestal.

After several revolutions at a trot, draw him in toward the pedestal, give him the "Ready" cue and urge him to "Step Up" before he comes to a halt.

Release him to step down and repeat the sequence. Longe him in to the pedestal and cue him to "Step Up" as he is still trotting. Praise him for even a small increase in lift and give him a breather. Most horses will begin to add lift as they increase their momentum.

Working into pressure as we covered in Pedestal Training can help to develop a full and balanced Rear from the Half Rear. Send the horse into the corner with more pressure and add the verbal cues used to develop the Half Rear.

The horse must lift his head to sustain the Rear. Some horses will follow the handler's uplifted hand or the tip of the whip held in

The rear begins by speeding up mounting the pedestal.

front of the nose as cues. Projecting more energy toward him may also help him stay up as will returning to the Climbing Wall. Balancing on the Wall helps to reduce the emotional component and helps him balance and build strength.

Staying Up—Circus Style

In the circus, the Rear is perfected with a pair of trained assistants holding long lead ropes attached to each side of a horse's halter. The head trainer stands in front of the horse and raises the tip of both his whips as the assistants on each side raise their hands in a gesture that mimics a horse rearing. Positioned slightly to the rear of the horse's shoulder, the assistants lightly check his forward movement, which gently urges him to sustain the Rear.

Encouraging the Hind Leg Walk

The Hind Leg Walk adds forward movement while the horse is Rearing. The trainer may keep the horse's attention by raising his whips at nose level in front of the horse as he takes a step back. A light touch with a longe whip at his heels may be used to encourage the horse to take a step.

If the horse has been taught to target a pedestal, place it slightly out of reach and ask him for a Rear. He may realize he has to take a step forward to reach it.

It is normal for a horse to first drop his front feet to the ground and then step up on the pedestal. This is creating a simple Behavior Chain by linking Rear and stepping up onto the pedestal. Over time he will learn not to drop until reaching the pedestal.

Enframing the Neck for Correct Position

The horse will be rigged with a snaffle bit and surcingle. A strap approximately 10" long with a ring on one end and snap on the other is clipped to the center ring of the surcingle and adjusted so the ring is in the hatchet mark or dip in front of the horse's withers. Clip a long, lightweight rope or light web longe line to the

bit ring on the far (off) side of the horse's bit. Run the line back through the ring in front of the withers and then forward through the left or near bit ring to be held in the handler's hand.

This is called enframing the neck. Adjust the long rein so the horse slightly tucks his nose. When cued to rear, his head and neck will be in position to help him raise his withers and balance. He can be checked lightly during the Rear to urge him to stay up.

Side reins can be used to create the tuck. Keep the lead rope on to pull the horse down if he goes too high and is in danger of going over backwards. This is one more tool in your bag of tricks to help achieve a balanced Rear and Hind Leg Walk.

This is a typical rigging to help in "Enframing the neck."

The "Fighting" Rear

The Fighting Rear or bicycling is when the horse paws the air while rearing. It is easiest to obtain with stallions but we have also taught it to geldings and mares.

As the horse rears, the handler engages him with whip gestures or by touching the forelegs. The horse will generally strike back at the whip in a (hopefully) playful manner. This is a delicate move and should be done in a way the horse won't resent it. Respect a horse's play drive but don't push him hard enough that he will strike or fight. This would most likely occur with stallions. Use a different set of cues than for the regular Rear.

High Rigging

High Rigging is similar to having assistants on the sides of the horse.

Our barn has a high roof in the center aisle and we attached two rings about 12 ft. from the floor on each side of the aisle. A long, lightweight rope is run through the ring on the left and continues across the ceiling and down through the ring on the right side of the aisle way. The rope has clips on the ends that will be snapped to the side rings on a horse's halter. This arrangement allows the handler to adjust the length and hold both ropes in his left hand.

Position the horse several feet back from the raised rings. Place a pedestal in the center of the aisle and ask the horse to walk forward and step up while staying in a straight line. The high rigging is like cross ties except the handler can give and take up slack or tension. Slowly and incrementally, teach the horse to rear and walk forward to target and land (front feet) on the pedestal. In the beginning you may need to touch him lightly with the whip, either on his shoulder or perhaps on the side of his neck as you establish cues for him. Over time, you may diminish the touch to a

Monet in a photo shoot.

gesture backed with a verbal cue.

High Rigging should be used as an aid only and not a primary method to teach the Rear.

Full instructions are included in the DVD *"Teaching the Rear".*

Retrieving the Big Ball

Herding the ball is a creative learning challenge that develops boldness and creates a can-do attitude. With encouragement a horse's can-do attitude evolves into a want-to-do work ethic.

Teaching a horse to roll and herd the Big Ball can really bring out the brainpower of some horses as they develop the ability to control and predict its direction. This seems to demonstrate a higher developed intelligence than horses merely responding to a cue. Learning to anticipate or predict the path of a ball requires a clever equine mind.

Herding the ball is easiest for an inquisitive and outgoing horse with a desire to learn and interact. A horse can't be forced to herd a ball—the human must be a motivational and effective teacher!

Equipment

- Large horse-appropriate inflatable ball

Benefits

- You can actually play with your horse

- Encourages a horse to lower his head and stretch his back

  Appeals to a horse's natural curiosity
- Develops the herding instinct

- A horse learns to target an object with his nose

Cues
- **Vocal cue** is "Get It" and then "Bring It Here" or simply "Here"

Dos and Navegador are team players!

- **Proximity cue** can be very close or as far away as your horse will respond

- **Physical cue** is drawing attention to the object, usually by movement

Strategy

Herding the ball is similar to teaching a young horse to track a cow in early stages of mounted training. A cow will predictably move away when the horse gets inside her comfort zone. The horse will predictably follow the cow to investigate it.

The Big Ball is an interactive toy and should never be used to scare or desensitize a horse. It's tempting to let horses play with a Big Ball but they will ultimately find a way to kill it, which will make it almost impossible to teach him to herd it, let alone facilitate learning.

Tracking a Big Ball is great for horses of all ages, but it is especially easy to teach a young horse to herd it.

We allow the horse to become accustomed to the ball by placing it in a stationary position while we pay no attention to it. The handler can roll the ball as he moves around the barn or roll it while feeding to accustom the horse to it. It is never to be bounced or rolled toward him in an attempt to desensitize him. It should always be moved by the handler and away from the horse. This will lessen his fear and increase his curiosity.

The key to teaching this rather complex behavior is to break it down into small components and teach each one as a separate trick.

It is important to introduce this lesson in an error-free manner. This means you should not allow the horse to bump the ball with his chest or legs. He needs to learn that the only acceptable way to engage with the ball is by using his nose. A horse simply cannot develop the skill

The yearling Tabajara is introduced to the big ball in a controlled situation. Allen slowly rolls it away from him as he keeps Taba close by.

Allen stays right with Taba to entice him to touch the ball. In Tricks of Engagement, both horse and human must stay engaged.

Taba's response is perfect as he reaches out when Allen tells him to "Push It".

The telescoping of the neck builds muscle, relaxation and begins to prepare the horse's muscle memory for his future athletic career. This is a good example of a gymnastic exercise that will benefit the horse his entire life.

Allen changes positions and urges Taba to "bring it here".

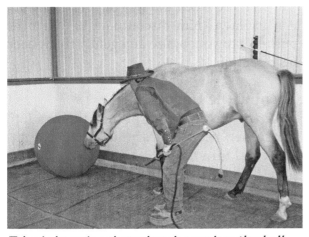

Taba is learning that when he pushes the ball into the corner, it changes direction. He followed the ball through the change in direction so he could continue down the straightaway.

to maneuver and guide a ball unless he learns to use only his nose.

It works well to lead the horse (halter and lead) as we control the ball. This is a simple task that can help him begin to track the big ball around the stall or training area.

Some horses really get into the spirit of rolling the ball and become aggressive and push or slam it. Slow down and keep him in control and slow him so he doesn't lose his concentration. We teach herding the Big Ball in a rectangular double stall 15 by 30 feet as this gives two long walls to keep the ball rolling straight. Food treats are usually helpful.

Steps

Place a halter and lead on the horse and carry a whip butt first or reversed in your hand.

Place the horse parallel to the wall in the schooling area, and your own body close to the horse. The ball will be next to the wall and you will halt with horse in hand approximately three feet from the ball. Approach it very slowly and lightly nudge the ball forward with the butt end of a whip (or a short stick). Roll it only a couple of feet. Encourage the horse's natural curiosity by keeping the ball just out of his reach until you halt.

Repeat the process until he will stop the correct distance from the ball and reach out to investigate or touch it with his nose. Use the halter and lead to urge him to lower his head a little more. In lowering his head, his nose will automatically touch the ball, perhaps with a little help from you. When he touches the ball, carefully nudge it forward.

Praise the horse and stroke his neck for reassurance as though he had made the ball move. Wait a few seconds and repeat the process. Bend forward at the waist and nudge the

Taba followed the ball out of the last corner and through the next. He gained enough confidence to use his nose to direct it. This develops determination to complete the job at hand.

ball again. Your interest in the ball will usually get the horse interested in it also.

We want to make him wonder why the ball moved away when he gets close. As the horse's curiosity grows he will predictably reach forward and sniff the ball or even touch it with his nose. This is allowed only at the halt and from a short distance away. Encourage him to lower his head as he reaches for the ball. Your body posture may cause him to mimic your position and actions.

If he either smells or touches the ball with his nose only, reward him quickly with a stroke on the neck or even a small food treat. Offer the treat very close to the ball so the horse begins to associate the treat with the ball.

Repeat the process with the appropriate number of repetitions for your horse. Generally four or five repetitions are plenty. Allow the horse time to chew and swallow each food treat between repetitions.

Walk close to the horse's shoulder to monitor and control his every move. As the horse becomes reliable in pushing the ball and stops the correct distance from it, you may try taking the halter off. Try standing just a little further away, either to the side or slightly in front of the ball.

Some horses enjoy rolling the ball back and forth between the two of you. Try it but if it frightens him discontinue it. When he pushes it to you, praise and gently roll it back his direction.

Turning the Corner

When the horse has pushed the ball into the corner, he must learn how to get it unstuck and turn the corner. To do this, he will place his head to the side of the ball and nudge it with the side of his nose instead of the front part of his nose.

This is a HUGE leap of progress and is how a horse learns, not only to guide a ball but also to push it with his nose. When the ball gets stuck in a corner, stand a few feet around

Navegador guides the direction of the big ball with concentration and determination to "Bring it Here" to Allen. He has developed a "Want to do Work Ethic".

the corner in the direction he needs to move it through the corner. Encourage him verbally and as he pushes it out of the corner, it will come toward you, reward him as when he rolled the ball in a straight line along the long wall.

With practice a horse will become adept at negotiating the ball around the corner and on down the next wall. At this point you may be able to let the horse handle the ball completely on his own.

We use a double-sized stall as a schooling area or an unobstructed aisle way of the barn. We place a beanbag in each corner so the ball will not get stuck. We want to set him up for success in the beginning. Use an object big enough to round out the corner so the ball will bounce and keep moving when it hits it.

We set a pedestal in the center of the rectangular schooling area about six feet away from the end wall. This will keep the ball more or less on track to automatically go into the corner. We want to make it easy for him to push the ball along and through the corners in a self-propelled manner. You may stand at one end of the schooling area, set the ball in motion and send the horse after it. He should be able to nudge it through the corners and bring it back along the other long wall to you.

Many horses seem to make very little progress the first few days or even after a week of work. Have patience, as we have never seen a horse fail (at some point) to suddenly begin pushing the ball around as if he has been herding it his entire life.

Further instructions are included in the DVD *"Shaping Behaviors I".*

Ibn Hasan and Allen herd the ball. This was Hasan's third or fourth ride. He is concentrating on herding the ball, a trick that he already knew and thinks nothing of his coach, Allen being on him rather than beside him.

The Trick Horse Companion

Retrieving an Object

Retrieving is a Trick of Engagement. The horse must want to engage and there is absolutely no other way to get him to retrieve otherwise. While some horses do naturally pick up objects to play with or to draw attention, getting a reliable retrieve is a separate trick. Even the best natural retriever can usually benefit from structured teaching for reliability.

Fetching an object is certainly not a natural behavior for most horses as it is for dogs. While it is common to see horses pick up objects and move them around, it is a different matter to get them to retrieve on cue. He must decide to do it of his own free will.

Folks often ask if teaching a horse to retrieve will make a mouthy horse even mouthier, and usually the answer is "no."

The retrieve can be useful or for fun.

Food treats must be used to teach and sustain motivation.

Equipment

- A dedicated baseball cap

- A handkerchief or small towel

- A specially modified Frisbee or other useful object, with a grip tab attached

- A Toss and Retrieve ball

Benefits

- A great trick to help build simple Behavior Chains, retrieving teaches a horse to accept an object in his mouth and think at the same time, helping to prepare him for carrying a bit

- Retrieving increases attention span and willing interaction with the handler

Cues

- **Vocal cue is** "Pick it up" or "Pick up the_____".
- **Proximity cue** (at first) is placing the

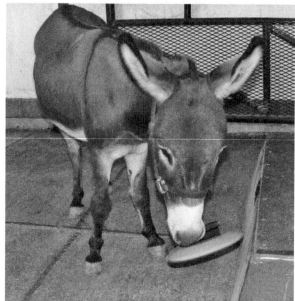

A lot of naturally mouthy horses get less mouthy when they learn behaviors such as retrieving, as it is an outlet for the behavior. Some horses absolutely will not pick up an object so it is best to choose a horse that is a little mouthy.

object in a horse's mouth. Later the cue can be to stand very close or as far away as your horse will respond.

- **Physical cue** is drawing attention to the object or pointing the horse's nose (with the halter).

Steps

We start with a dedicated cap that has our smell. The stiff brim allows us to place it into the horse's mouth and help him hold it there. Touch the cap to the horse's mouth to see if he is interested enough to nibble at it or even take it in his mouth. If he does, give the bridge cue of "Good" and offer a cookie immediately. Most horses, if they have an inclination to be mouthy, will catch on very quickly as it is an easy way to get a cookie without much work.

At first, if the horse will even let his nose be guided to touch the object, use the verbal cue "pick it up" each and every time he touches or lips the object.

A few repetitions per session are all most horses can stay focused for. We like to end a session while the horse is still interested rather than when the focus begins to wane. This will help his enthusiasm carry over to the next session and he will be eager to earn a treat.

If he will hold the cap (or other object) in his mouth for even a few seconds, scratch his withers and praise him. Stop scratching immediately if he drops it—which undoubtedly he will do.

We want him to associate the nice scratching with having it in his mouth. This exchange may go on for quite a few sessions. If he seems to stop trying, walk away from him and leave him alone for 10 or 15 minutes.

When he starts holding the object for a few seconds more, take it from his mouth and give him verbal praise as you deliver a treat. You have about two seconds to reward him or he won't make the connection. Even if the progress seems incredibly slow, continue on. When you get to the point he will let you exchange the object for a cookie, you will have made a big breakthrough. Until he understands the exchange, do not try to move.

When he is reliable at exchanging the object, do not give him a cookie if he drops it. Say something like "no" or "no dropping" and ignore him, pause for a few seconds, then repeat. Work to perfect your own timing so you can trade a cookie quickly for the object.

When the horse is proficient at holding the object for incrementally longer periods (seconds not minutes), place the object on a pedestal or other slightly raised surface and ask him to "Pick It Up." The ground or floor is too far away, and placing it higher makes it easy for him to "find" the object.

Stay close to him when you ask him to pick up the object, as this will help him keep his focus. As he becomes reliable at picking the object up from a close location, begin asking him to take a step toward you while holding it—just a step. You may need to attach a lead rope to help him swing his head to the side while holding the object. Increase a step each day as you ask him to "come here." At first, he may only be able to turn his head a few inches from a straight ahead position to hand you the object without losing his concentration. What may seem to you like a reasonable increase may be beyond the horse's ability at this time. This is a difficult concept.

When he is confirmed in picking the object up from a close location, incrementally increase the distance. Each session may bring an increase in distance and if not, go back to the point that he is able to do it. Once a horse is confirmed in picking it up, ask him to "Come Here," or "Bring It Back," or whatever you decide to call it. If the horse drops it, do not give him a cookie and say "no" or "no dropping," ignore him, and then repeat the request.

Gradually increase the distance he can pick up the object and bring it back.

We can throw a Frisbee for our horses while they are on a pedestal and cue them to go get it, bring it back and Spanish Walk to the Pedestal or even Rear to it before handing it back to us.

Food Tied in a Cloth

An easy method to get a horse who is not particularly curious or mouthy to open his mouth and pick up an object is to tie a small amount of food in a soft cloth. Use enough food to make a packet about the size of a golf ball and tie the cloth in a knot or use a piece of string to tie it closed. Halter the horse and attach a lead. We usually sit down on a pedestal facing the horse and show him the packet

Rafiq is interested in the sock filled with grain.

containing the food. We set it down on the pedestal right in front of him. Most horses will curiously nudge the packet trying to figure out how to reach the food. Often we need to be creative in our attempts to get the horse to actually bite down on the packet the first few times. When the packet is actually in the mouth, his saliva helps the smell and taste of the food to permeate the cloth and he will readily bite at it.

The challenge is to get him to hold it or play with it and exchange it for a treat. We may put a finger between his lips to urge him to open his mouth and release it. We have a food reward ready to immediately replace the packet that he can actually chew. It may be difficult for a horse to understand he must give up the packet to get a reward. Try to be gentle when exchanging the packet for the treat so as not to violate his trust. Be satisfied if he will only pick up the packet for a moment before dropping it in search of a reward.

When he is confirmed in picking the object up from a close location, incrementally set the packet down farther away from you and toward the right side of the pedestal (assuming you are on the horse's left side).

We would like the horse to swing his head to the right and pick up the packet. As he does so, we use the lead rope to ever so gently bring his head back in our direction while he is holding the packet in his mouth. We then make the exchange for the food treat and wait until he has had plenty of time to chew and swallow before moving on.

It is a huge stretch for most horses to be able to pick up an object, turn and take a step to exchange it for a treat. If too great a distance is asked early on, it may set him back considerably in his progress. A foot of distance he carries an object is a good increase per day.

We may spend several days with several sessions per day before we see much progress.

Gradually we will be able to set the packet on the far side of the pedestal and get the horse to actually take a step to reach it and possibly exchange it for a treat. Getting him to move his feet without dropping the food packet takes a lot of concentration and is new level of behavior for a horse.

Moving on to the Frisbee

As the horse becomes proficient at picking up the food packet, we progress to using a modified Frisbee. It may take several sessions until the horse will associate picking up the Frisbee with the gripper tab with the cue "pick it up."

Use a Frisbee that another horse has picked up as it will probably have crumbs of treats on the gripper tab to make it smell and taste like the food. We often use black licorice as a food treat and a slightly chewed/wet piece can be rubbed on the gripper tab (if your horse likes licorice). You may try other tasty snacks to entice the horse.

When the horse picks up the sock, be quick to gently exchange it for a treat.

As the horse learns to pick up the Frisbee, the distance may be increased in small degrees from the initial placement and where you sit or stand to exchange it for a food reward. End each session while the horse is still eager and before he loses interest.

Verbal encouragement at each individual step can help keep your horse's interest and focus. When he will actually go and pick up a tossed object a few feet we may say "GO—pick it up," then "Pick it up" when his head drops and "Bring it here'" or just "Here" as he returns with it. It will help to encourage him verbally by telling him "Good" as he is walking away from you to pick up the object and also to help him to stay focused as he brings

It may take some time for the horse to pick something up from the ground.

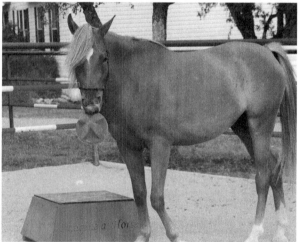

The horse must be introduced to each new object to be retrieved. Rafiq is learning to swing his head to the side while holding the ball. Taking a step with it is a big accomplishment.

it back. Your voice is his lifeline, his encouragement.

If he drops the object, tell him "No dropping" and repeat the sequence.

Include walkabout time between repetitions and allow him to enjoy his food treat.

Making a Basket

In addition to retrieving a Frisbee and handing it directly back to you, we teach retrieving a ball and placing it in a large bucket or basket.

The Retrieve takes on a completely new dimension because the horse must associate placement of the ball in the bucket with the delayed food reward after making the "basket".

Making a basket requires genuine thinking to accomplish.

Proceed teaching the horse to retrieve the ball as in teaching him to retrieve the Frisbee. There is one important difference–we never, not even once, accept the ball into our hands. From the beginning the horse brings the ball, it must be caught in a large 20 gallon muck bucket or he will not be able to make the association.

We enable him to target the bucket with the ball and then for weeks, maybe months, move it to help him "make a basket" in the bucket. This behavior generally takes many, many repetitions before the horse is even remotely aware that the requirements are different than bringing the Frisbee (or any other object) back to the handler.

Common Problems

- A horse may become pushy when offered treats in quick succession Some horses need more walkabout time to eat the treat and stay interested in getting another.

- A horse can lose interest quickly, so keep repetitions to just a few.

Tips

- Understand your horse's maximum concentration time.

- Fetching an object directly in front of the horse is completely different than if he is asked to fetch to the left or right. Each direction is taught separately. If a horse is pushed beyond

his understanding he will lose interest. Lessons can be frequent but short

- Keep your patience and focus.

- Not all horses are drawn to the same type of objects.

- Do not get frustrated with your horse's progress or lack thereof.

- A horse needs your support and engagement to stay motivated and focused.

- Each horse's progress is different.

- Do not leave the toys with a horse when he is not in school.

- Keep sessions short and put the toy away so it will be interesting next time.

- Dwell time between repetitions helps the horse to assimilate the lesson.

- Hand graze him or tie him between sessions.

- Let him watch other horses retrieve.

Further instructions are included in the DVDs *"Shaping Behaviors II".*

Fetching an object, such as this rubber ball with grips, is a complex behavior, so be patient during the learning process.

The Trick Horse Companion

Working "In The Round"

Modern Horsemanship from the Renaissance Period

In our modern world it is refreshing to realize many fine horsemen throughout the ages used sophisticated and effective horse training methods that were also kind and respectful to the horse.

Ancient Horsemanship

Renaissance trainer Antoine Pluvenile's book *"Le Menage Royal"* was published in 1633 and detailed the use of a single pillar in horse training. Pluvenile was one of the first since Xenophon in about 350 BC to see the horse as a sentient being. He was noted for his humane methods of treatment of the horse and used "gentling" rather than "breaking."

Visten gives a beautiful Spanish Walk in-hand.

"Of special value was his insistence on courtesy, sound judgment, patience and virtue" and consideration that the horse "must take pleasure in his work." Pluvenile as Royal Ecuyer to King Louis the 14th used and wrote of the single pillar but since, little has been written about how to incorporate pillars, either single or double, as a tool for horse training. The Vaqueros of California brought sophisticated training methods to American horse training, including the single pillar.

At Imagine a Horse, we use the ancient and classical single pillar to teach and perfect basic obedience as well as high school gaits such as the Spanish Walk, Passage and March steps. Here we call the pillar the Liberty Pole because it is the link between simple in-hand schooling to Liberty Training or work in which the horse has no attachment to the handler.

Such modern and legendary horsemen as Al Dunning and Mike Bridges are among trainers who incorporate use of a single pillar in their training although the name is different as Al calls it a Patience Pole and Mike calls it a Circus Pole. Nonetheless both see the value in incorporating training at the pole.

Horse Breaking on the Range

American ranch life in the early years necessitated the taming or breaking of the working ranch horse, who was ever in demand. Although the Vaquero methods of California turned out many a work of art in the finished

Odds Against Him

A sketch for the subtitle Horse Breaking on the Range from "California Hackamore" by Luis Ortega shows how the snubbing post was used.

bridle horse, the big cattle outfits of the plains had to make quicker work of breaking horses. The single pillar became the utilitarian snubbing post as a short cut to the more time consuming Vaquero methods. Horses were commonly tied to the post, snubbed down tight and sacked out with little regard for their wellbeing. The goal was simply to break the horse. Broncs, as they were often referred to, would be saddled while snubbed and often with one leg tied up they were mounted and ridden until they gave up bucking. Cowboys and ranch hands were used to a hard life and took their knocks in stride and the horses were expected to do the same. Untamed horses were cheap and easy to replace.

The Revolution in Horsemanship

In his book, *"The Revolution in Horsemanship,"* Dr. Robert M. Miller says the old ways of breaking horses have nearly been eradicated in our modern and enlightened society. Round pen schooling has become an accepted and more humane way of gentling a horse than harsher methods such as the snubbing post. Results are dramatically improved and usually quicker, too.

As the open range dwindled, cowmen such as Buster Welch began to utilize the round pen to finish training their cow horses and reined horses. They needed an alternative to galloping untrained horses in the open. The standard working 60-foot diameter round pen was quickly adapted because most horses could lope easily in this size enclosure.

Please note we are referring to finishing under saddle work, not other round pen methods. We do not condone the practice of running a horse in the round pen to the point of exhaustion until he "gives in" or "joins up" out of hopelessness.

The Liberty Pole has an effect similar to round penning as the horse has some freedom of movement.

Liberty Pole by Imagine A Horse
In the Renaissance period, the single wooden pillar had a horizontal groove with a lead rope loosely tied into the groove so that it could slip around the post as the horse circled. At our ranch the Liberty Pole is a 4 ½" diameter steel pipe, 7 ½ feet tall and has a 360° swivel at the top to attach a lead rope with a quick release snap. We use a 20' loose rope run through the ring (on the pole) initially so the handler can instantly yield slack if the horse panics or pulls back.

Training at any speed on a round track should be done in moderation even with a horse of full physical development, to avoid overstressing joints and tendons.

Using the Liberty Pole, Working in the "Round"

To establish movement around the pole, fasten the horse's (long) lead to the swivel and attach a second lead rope to the halter ring on the outside track and walk alongside of him. This is similar to having a handler on each side of the horse. As the horse understands the partial confinement of the pole and develops self-carriage and self-discipline, he can be attached directly to the pole and asked to move on his own. Put quick release snaps at both ends.

Over time he should allow himself to be directed around the pole with you in any position including on the inside track, beside him, in front, behind or while standing on the outside of the circle or track.

Changes of direction or half circles can be taught and even circles and figures-of-eight with the handler on the outside of the track. Voice aids and whip cues can help him through complete circles both moving away from the handler and also moving towards him.

When the handler is on the inside track, the horse will learn he must turn towards the handler while making a change of direction. If he attempts to make an outside turn, he will automatically be constricted by the rope. Inside turns are always preferred over allowing a horse to make an outside turn and turn his hind end to the handler. This is generally a sign of disrespect and evasion as he is temporarily out of the handler's vision.

Learning Patience

The Liberty Pole is also an acceptable way to teach a horse to patiently stand tied although it requires constant monitoring by the handler. He should be tied up close with a slip tie such as the Blocker Tie that can be attached to the swivel. Do not use the same length of rope as was used in working the horse on the pole. The slip tie is a nifty mechanism that gives slightly if a horse pulls back and eliminates the chance of damage to a horse's head and neck in a panic situation. Never leave a horse tied unattended in any circumstance and be sure that you always have a sharp pocketknife in the event you must free a horse quickly.

Preparing for the Spanish Walk

The Spanish Walk is a beautiful High School move in which a horse offers willing, generous and majestic steps with slow motion eloquence. We teach the Jambette, also called a Salute, as a basis for the Spanish Walk, which is a "trick of gait" or an amplification of one of the horse's natural gaits.

All breeds may be able to give a great Spanish Walk yet be mindful of each horse's conformation and how it may affect both his reach and lift. Some lift the leg high and straight out while others slightly arch the leg at the knee joint before the leg is straightened and extended. Either form is acceptable as long as the leg is straight as it hits the ground.

For the SW to be classically correct is should contain the same four beat cadence of a normal walk. However when a horse has an extremely strong diagonal reflex such as Navegador, you may see the SW become a two beat or diagonal walk. Equestrian Tact should be applied or in other words, consider your horse's natural abilities.

Allen is teaching Taba to move around the pole. The rope is always held by the handler in the early stages so that he can give and take very softly of the slack to maintain the young horse's confidence.

Most horses will easily move or even lift a front leg if tapped gently with a guider whip on the back of the forearm. Stand on the left side of the horse to cue the left leg and step to the right side to cue the right leg so that it is easy for the horse to understand the difference. We use "One" as the verbal cue for the left and "Two" as the cue for the right leg. We use these particular verbal cues so when the Jambette is later on shaped into the Spanish Walk, we can count cadence to encourage the horse to lift the legs. If you prefer not to use verbal cues, that's fine too.

At first, acknowledge and praise even the slightest lift of the leg. It may take your horse a few days or a week to offer a salute in which he actually lifts the leg. When the horse will reliably give you the Jambette on the left, teach it on the right side also.

Learning Spanish Walk at the Liberty Pole

Adding forward movement with the hindquarters can be difficult if too much attention is focused on the lift or height of the front leg. Impress on the horse from the beginning, forward movement is the major goal and lift and height is secondary. Lift and height will come as the horse learns to drive forward from the hindquarters and becomes more relaxed.

Attach the horse to the Liberty Pole and attach an additional lead to the outside of his halter. Cue him to lift his left leg ("One") as he learned with the Jambette. Give him plenty of time to respond as this is a complex request at first. When he lifts his leg, tell him "Good" and at the same time urge him forward. Always walk with the horse as it will help him to understand that forward movement is desired.

The handler can send the horse off in a circle while staying inside the track and under the swivel on the Liberty Pole.

The Trick Horse Companion

As the horse progresses in his schooling, Allen steps to the outside of the track and asks Dos to come toward him. This is called working into pressure and helps to increase a horse's confidence.

The slightest initial effort should be generously rewarded for the horse to begin to understand forward movement must be coupled with the high leg lift. Ask for only one step with the leg raised and walk on. Make a complete revolution on the pillar and when you reach the "mark" or first place you asked for the step, halt for a few seconds and ask again.

Work only on one side and with one leg at a time in the first few sessions. At this point, do not switch to the other front leg and do not ask for a Big (SW) Step from alternate legs—only ask for one step at a time followed by a strong and vigorous walk forward after the initial "Big Step."

Let the focus be on just one step, on one side. It is common to spend a few days or even a week or more focusing on the same leg. When the horse becomes reliable and will offer the Big Step (still one side) every time he is asked, only then is it time to reverse directions and teach from the other side and with the other leg.

A good Spanish Walk step is good extension of the cued front leg AND a step forward, still one side (leg) only at two opposite locations on the pillar. After the cadenced walk is confirmed on one side, begin the process over again on the opposite side with the other front leg.

As the horse gains the ability to give the correct response on each side, in each direction, you can shift the cadence by asking for a Spanish step at shorter intervals around the pillar. Most horses will begin to offer a few steps of real Spanish Walk with alternat-

With Navegador between the pillar and Allen, it is like having a schooling assistant!

We use a mat as a target to help a horse understand transitions of gait. Here Allen asked Dos to halt on the mat and then to strike off in a March step.

ing legs when they are ready, physically and mentally. This is a complex task, and the handler's patience and equestrian tact are really important.

Spanish Walk on the Straight

Position the horse close to, and parallel to a wall or safe fence. As you walk him along the barrier ask for the Big Step at the same location each time. This helps him understand and anticipate a request is coming.

The teaching steps are the same as on the Liberty Pole.

Place or Mark

Teach transitions of gait and the halt on the pole by giving the horse a "mark" or predetermined spot at which he will make the transitions. Use a rubber mat large enough for the horse to stand on with all four feet. This will keep him engaged and help him focus on moving forward toward the "mark" in anticipation of the change. Give him a reason to step on the mat such as a food treat or praise. The mat can be used on the Liberty Pole or on the straight.

Counting Cadence

There are several variations we employ in counting cadence with a horse. It is up to you and your horse which variation you go with as long as it is done the same every time in a way that doesn't confuse him. Be consistent with cues and cadence and reward for improvement.

When the horse is confirmed in offering a proper extension of the cued front leg AND can take a step forward, begin asking for a Spanish Walk step or Big Step every fourth step. At this point, counting cadence for the horse can be a huge help. Walk next to the horse and ask for the Big Step on every fourth step. "One" becomes the Big Step, two, three and four are regular walk strides. As the horse completes the cadence, repeat it. Most horses begin to understand the request to take a Big Step every fourth step (same side) within a couple of sessions. After the cadenced walk is confirmed on one side, begin the process over again on the opposite side with the other front leg.

When the horse is reliable with a Big Step every fourth step, ask for it every third step, then every second step and so on. During this process, most horses will begin to offer a few steps of real Spanish Walk. Each horse will begin to offer big steps with alternating legs when he is ready, physically and mentally.

It takes time to condition for more than a few steps of Spanish Walk. When the horse has learned alternating legs, limit the number of steps you ask for. Start with two steps, (left and right) and walk forward. Return to the designated mark and repeat the two Spanish Walk steps. Increase the number of steps one at a time so the horse doesn't become frustrated or dull.

Some horses respond best when asked for alternate legs or left, right, left (One, Two, One) with a few regular steps between. If this is what you choose, always count the same number of steps between the alternate side Big Steps. One, Two, One and (for example) three or four steps before repeating the Big Steps.

The Three Step

When the horse has learned a cadenced or counted walk, the Three Step is yet another alternative. This is a left, regular, regular, right. In other words the third step is a Big Step, another three regular steps and a Big Step on the opposite side. One, step, step, Two, step, step, One, step, step and so on.

The Three Step is often used with exhibition performance horses while they are still in strength training for the "real" Spanish Walk. If doing a demonstration with your own horse before his training is perfected, be confident the Three Step is a legitimate way to show him off.

Developing Reach at the Cleat Board

Position the horse a few steps back from the Cleat Board and walk him forward as you cue him for either the Three Step or alternate legs. Most horses soon start reaching for the board as they offer the Big Steps. This increases reach and lift with a target they already understand.

Mounted Spanish Walk

Make the transition to the mounted Spanish Walk gradually.

When transitioning, add a rider as the handler walks beside the horse and counts cadence. This can be done on the straight or in front of the Cleat Board. Obviously this is too dangerous to try on the Liberty Pole.

Using the cleat board as a target helps Uno to extend his reach.

At first, the handler should cue the horse as the rider remains passive. Rider cues can be added gradually and also gradually eliminated. As the horse raises his left leg, the rider touches him at the girth with the opposite leg as it is used to gain an extended mounted walk. As the horse lifts his leg, a mild upward lift on the same side is used with the rein.

Rafiq mounts the two-tier pedestal.

The Trick Horse Companion

Liberty Training I

Liberty Training is a great way to spend quality educational time with a horse and is useful to enhance the education of a young horse not yet physically mature enough to ride. Obedience, reliability, self-carriage and self-confidence are all increased with Liberty Training as the horse learns to respond to cues without a lead. The freedom of movement keeps the horses involved and energized in their work. Liberty Training can work to hone to perfection your horse's response whether he's working at a distance or walking next to you.

At Imagine A Horse, the Liberty patterns interspersed with tricks and behavior chains make for an intricate Circus-Style Act. The liberty movement between the tricks is like the silence between the notes that results in a musical melody. A Circus-Style Liberty Act is simply developing the intricacy from basic work, and adding a couple of horses and some showmanship!

Liberty Training can aid in tasks as simple as your horse walking with you, untethered. The goal is to develop through Liberty schooling a horse that will stay with you and work with you reliably through mental attachment independently, without the physical security of a lead.

"Walk With Me"

It is both fun and functional to have a horse "walk with" you without a lead. Executing the halts, turns and simple patterns he has learned will give him an incentive to "walk with" you. Offer praise or even a food treat as an added bonus to stay with you. Walking beside you slowly through patterns is a comfortable place for a horse to be; he has leadership, companionship AND it is easy. If he becomes detached from you, send him out to work at a quick pace for a minute or two before you ask him to come back and "walk with" you. Most horses will happily walk next to you rather than do laps in the pen!

At this time, when your horse comes to you rather than trotting the perimeter, it is a good time to introduce a verbal cue such as "come" or "here" followed by a food treat. The verbal cue of "here" can also be transferred to a whistle cue that can be used on the trail if you are accidentally separated from your horse.

"Big Ben" working solo.

Boullet is learning to take direction from the whips and Sue's body language.

The (Almost) Lost Art of the Square Pen

Long before round pens became popular, the square pen or corral was a staple of horse training. The corners of a square pen offer valuable training opportunities as a horse can be taught to walk straight lines, stop, back, turn corners towards the handler and maneuver around obstacles, all at liberty.

In a pen of 45 x 45 feet square no easy escape routes are available to the horse. By instilling habitual compliance, a mental connection with the trainer can be called upon throughout the horse's life and utilized in all training endeavors.

The square pen is the best training area or aid for creating understanding and obedience at liberty. The small round pen will be introduced later.

Square pen work should first be done only at a walk. Letting a horse zoom around either a round pen or square pen actually plays into a horse's inherent nature of "flight" and does little or nothing to calm him or tire him. Slow, thoughtful work engages the horse's mind and helps to create interaction, understanding and a mental attachment to the handler.

Liberty Schooling in a square pen requires thoughtful positioning of the handler's body and utilization of the correct tools such as horse-friendly guider whips. Imagine a Horse Guiders are flexible whips with a soft snap and ball on the end that enables the handler to touch a horse for direction and not sting him.

In Liberty work we always use two whips—a guider to control direction and a short or long longe whip for movement or impulsion of the horse. Face the horse's left side at a distance of about 10 feet, with the short guider in the left hand in a horizontal (neutral) position and the longe whip in the right hand and behind the horse's rump.

Teach the horse to move forward in the square pen at a walk by flicking the longe whip at his feet or rump, just as you would in a round pen, but push him deep into the corners rather than letting him cut the corners. Teach the same lesson on the opposite side.

Corners Create the Halt

The first lesson in the halt on cue is to move the horse forward in a straight line along the wall or fence and as he reaches the corner, block his forward movement and use the corner as a barrier for him and ask him to halt or

The whip positions help him understand the request to turn.

"whoa". A horse will usually understand this method quickly because it is his natural inclination to halt in the corners. When he halts in the corner, let him have a few seconds of dwell time (release) as a reward and then direct him to "walk" again. Repeat this sequence in both directions until the horse will reliably halt when asked in each corner of the pen from either direction.

Take Away Ground

One important concept to impress upon the horse when training at liberty is the handler controls the ground he stands on or passes over. If a horse misbehaves it can be a powerful rebuke if he is stopped immediately and made to back in a straight line. This is taking away the ground he controlled while he was disobedient. The trainer must convince the horse he may only pass over it IF he is mannerly, respectful and obedient to the cues.

Inside Turns

The corners of the square pen or corral offer a perfect place to instill the good habit of always turning toward the handler. It is not allowable for any horse (or foal) to turn his backside toward the handler.

Ask the horse to move into the corner of the pen as when teaching the halt in the corners. Guide him into the corner with the whip at his rear but as he reaches the corner (barrier) take a step toward his head to block his movement and at the same time, reach with the shorter whip under the outer side of the his chin to capture the attention of his outside eye as you continue to ask him to walk forward. The action (and intention) is to encourage him to turn toward you as you block any other option. As he turns toward you and begins to walk off, praise him and take the pressure to move off of him temporarily by letting him move at his own pace. Repeat this exercise in both directions until it is an automatic response for the horse to always turn toward you. We add the verbal cue "Turn" each time we ask him to turn.

Turning toward the handler is beneficial as it teaches the horse to look at you with each

Boullet mirrors Sue's body language.

eye separately and then with both eyes (and both sides of his brain) as he faces you while turning. The practice of turning toward you helps him to develop agility with both sides of his body.

Our horses are often handled in a constant state of Liberty Training. Instead of a physical attachment such as a lead rope or longe line, we strive to create mental and emotional attachments through meaningful exercises. We like to say foals raised in this manner are like kids growing up in the circus—they think everyone can juggle or, in this case, work at liberty.

As the horse becomes proficient at moving as directed in either direction, halting on cue and making turns toward you and continuing on, increase the speed to a trot and include walk/trot transitions and turns in the corners.

Simple Patterns

If two pedestals are placed in the pen a few feet from the corners, the horse can be guided through a figure-eight pattern around the pedestals. This is actually a half-turn around each pedestal with a cross over in the middle. As he becomes proficient at making the figure eight pattern he can also be taught to circle around a pedestal in each direction and even to circle it two or three times as requested.

To teach this, place a pedestal in the corner of the pen approximately 4 to 6 feet from the fence and begin to ask the horse to walk around or circle it as he comes out of a corner turn. Our horses respond to the verbal cue of "Turn" for a simple or half-turn and "Again" which means to complete the additional half of the circle all the way around the pedestal.

It is usually necessary to use a long, light lead rope to guide the horse through the figure-of-eight pattern initially. Some horses can easily cross the center line and change directions and others will be unnerved when asked to cross over the middle. The act of changing views or switching eyes can take gentle guidance for the horse to become comfortable and accepting.

The natural barrier of the corner, combined with whip cues, help Boullet to make turns to the inside or toward the handler.

Boullet learned to make a circle around the pedestal.

This simple set of patterns can become the foundation for a Circus-style Liberty Act or to simply increase the level of compliance that your horse will offer.

Working into Pressure

Corners of the square pen can be used to teach a unique concept we call "working into pressure." This is the first step in being able to "send" a horse to a particular pedestal at liberty. This valuable technique is different than teaching a horse to physically move away from pressure as is the case in most horse training. Working into pressure enhances boldness while creating obedience, a great concept for a working or sport horse! The horse will learn to think and to comprehend your intention and then act appropriately, not merely react by freezing in place, shutting down or running away.

The horse needs to know pedestal basics before moving on to this exercise. After he has been taught to mount the pedestal (with at least his two front feet), place a pedestal in the corner of the pen at an angle and five to six feet from where the two sides meet. Ask the horse to trot into the corner and "turn" toward you. Motivate him to hustle and, as he turns toward you, back up a step or two and ask him to "Step Up" onto the pedestal facing you. Turning toward you and then stepping up must be presented to him as his only option and the only way that the pressure on him will be released. During the first few repetitions, if the horse doesn't understand the request or is nervous, lead him to the pedestal and ask him to "Step Up" to demonstrate your request and then proceed.

Introducing the Small Round Pen

Having learned the primary elements of Liberty Training in a square pen, the progression will be to move to a small round pen of approximately 30 to 40 feet in diameter.

The lessons from the square pen are basically the same; however, the handler no longer has the advantage of corners to help control the horse's natural inclination to bolt or scoot away, either playfully or disobediently.

Utilizing the round pen in liberty work is not the same as running or free longeing

As Sue blocks Boullet's movement, he seeks his "release" by turning and mounting the pedestal. This is an example of working into pressure.

a horse until he gives up or tires and comes to you. The saying "When the blood starts to flow, the thinking starts to go" aptly describes the mental state of most horses when they are forced to run in a round pen. This type of thoughtless activity will elevate a horse's heart rate and cause an adrenaline surge that can last as long as 20 minutes. Elevated heart rate, respiration and adrenalin levels are counterproductive to learning.

There is certainly a place in horse training, especially with stock types and horses that haven't been handled a lot, for round pen techniques. We like the "Bonder" by Marv Walker the best. We have used his techniques many times in ground training. Herein we are devoted to training the domestically raised horse that has been handled his entire life and is considered to be a companion rather than a stock animal.

Pedestals can be positioned in the small round pen to help a horse learn both timing and accuracy in response to cues.

To teach a horse to reverse directions, a pedestal can be positioned about three feet from the pen's perimeter to create a narrow gap that the horse will go through before he is cued to reverse direction. This will naturally make it easier for him to make a turn around the pedestal than to duck back in behind the pedestal after he reverses. It is common for horses to turn back quickly and not come around the pedestal because they anticipate pressure from the handler.

There are several ways to urge the horse to come towards the center of the ring and

Boullet's intense focus is apparent.

actually turn around the pedestal. If he has been taught to come to a mat as his "place," it can be positioned within easy sight just past the turn around point at the end of the pedestal.

As he begins to make the small half circle to reverse, call him to his "place," reward him and send him in the correct direction with minimal pressure. The horse will understand the changes of direction easier if the steps are broken into small requests.

Later, when another horse is added to begin pattern work, one horse can stand on his "place" on the mat or pedestal and the second horse can be taught changes of direction. At this point an assistant (if available) could stand on the outside perimeter of the ring to raise and point a guider at the horse's nose to encourage him to make the inside turn around the pedestal.

Large Figure Eight or Change Through the Center

To create a change of direction between two pedestals, the rubber mat can be placed near the center of the small round pen and two pedestals opposite each other. The horse can be called to the center to "hit his mark" on the rubber mat, then sent on in the opposite direction. Crossing through the center should be taught at a walk initially to keep the horse calm. As his confidence grows he may be asked to make the change at a trot and proceed on to the canter. When the change over is done at the canter, the horse automatically changes leads as he crosses through the center and the bend in his body changes.

Serpentines

To teach a serpentine or weave pattern, place several pedestals approximately eight feet apart (in a row) and six feet from the perimeter of the ring. In order for the horse to understand the dynamics of executing a ser-pentine around three (or more) pedestals, he must learn to come to and go away from the handler. The mat or "place" will be in front of the handler on the inside of the line of pedestals. The handler will urge the horse to come to him as the horse passes between the (first) two pedestals and hit his mark on the mat. From his position on the mat, he will send the horse on between the next two pedestals. This is an intricate concept that will take consistent practice and considerable patience.

The Serpentine can be repeated in the opposite direction in the same manner or sequence. The rubber mats can be moved as needed or several mats can be used. The momentary pause on the mat and perhaps praise or a food treat before he is cued to move on will encourage him and help keep his stress level low.

Serpentines can be taught in an error-free manner if an assistant is available to lead the horse through the serpentine while the handler remains in the center of the ring and calls cues and offers direction with the guider whips. Training with an assistant can streamline the learning process.

The Waltz

The Waltz is an interesting and beautiful maneuver often seen in circus performances. Basically the Waltz is a very small circle that when done correctly is a pirouette on the hind legs.

One method to teach the Waltz is to accustom the horse to following his nose around his tail in a tight turn. A long lead line is attached to the halter and draped around his rear end to help him make a small circle. Be gentle with the touch on the lead so the horse will learn to follow a soft feel of the rope and keep his body straight through the turn. He should be taught to make a beginning pirouette with his entire body, not a sharp turn.

A verbal cue such as "Waltz" or "Around" can be added while the horse is learning on the lead. The horse should progress to the point that the rope can be laid across his back and against his neck at the same time as he is being asked for the turn. The feel of the rope against his neck will become the lightest of cues to make the turn. After some practice the rope can be wrapped very lightly around the horse's neck so he can learn to unwind it. Wrap the long soft rope around the horse's neck and walk with him to a designated mark and help him to unwind it in one revolution. Walk forward to the next mark and unwind another wrap. Soon he will be ready to Waltz at liberty, at which time whip cues can be added.

A complex behavior such as the Waltz is much more than a mere trick. It increases the horse's ability to focus his attention on the handler and indicates he is a willing partner.

The Waltz should be taught in both directions to create the most physical benefit.

Next we'll explore adding more horses to the mix to create a Liberty Act or better yet for the fun of a Circus in your own back yard!

Further instructions are included in the DVD *"Liberty Training I".*

The Trick Horse Companion

Liberty Training II

Circus Style Patterns with Multiple Horses

Let's look back at Liberty Training I and recap the skills that our horse(s) learned in the square pen, the Liberty Pole and the small round pen. Walk, trot, canter, whoa, gait transitions in a straight line with the corresponding whip and verbal cues, inside turns (towards the handler), change of directions, turns around an object such as a pedestal, circle the object, work into pressure and "come here" on cue. Coming to and standing on a mark as well as both small and large figures-of-eight and waltzing. By the time that these skills are confirmed in the horse, he should have developed a very good work ethic. All of these skills can be taught to a weanling or adolescent, just as easily and effectively as they can be taught to mature horses already under saddle. It's never too late to add Liberty Training to your trail horses' education.

Liberty Training helps to develop willing obedience in our companion horses AND it prepares performance horses for their Circus-Style Liberty Act. It increases a horse's responsiveness to the handler and also the handler's to the horse. One element often overlooked in traditional training disciplines is a horse's self-expression through movement as a reward and this will help keep him engaged in his work. A horse that enjoys his work will progress faster and further than one that is bored with mindless laps in a round pen or endless repetitions.

Liberty Training helps to create reliability and cooperation from the horse at a distance and demonstrates just how precise commu-

Imagine what is possible.

Rafiq and Uno working side by side. The outside horse is used to working with other horses but the inner horse is not. A longe line attached helps him keep his focus and understand the job.

nication can be. It helps a horse learn to stay focused on the handler on a level that simply cannot be achieved on a lead. It helps to sensitize a horse to our wishes and guidance, which is much different and we believe even more useful than most "desensitizing" techniques.

We do expose our horses to as many interesting and even unusual situations and objects as possible but don't focus excessively on desensitizing. Exposure to a potentially scary object by the way is NOT the same as scaring a horse with an object such as a flag (plastic bag on a stick) until he no longer reacts. If a human comes at a horse with an object he is scared of in order to desensitize him, why should he trust him? In our experience it is far more productive to develop the type of trust between a horse and a human that encourages willing obedience.

For Best Results at Liberty

A horse must know and consistently respond to his name. He should be able to understand (your) direction and cues and to recover from correction quickly with a positive frame of mind. Correction is NOT the same as punishment, which is reserved only

The horses are now going opposite directions. The inner or student horse still has the longe line.

for grave offenses. He should work reliably into pressure from the handler and not avoid directives by turning away. Horses are slow to think through requests but fast to react so we give him every opportunity to answer our requests by allowing him adequate response time and giving a preliminary vocal cue such as "Ready"? A horse should be called by name followed by a dwell time of a couple of seconds and then given a preparatory cue such as "Ready?" followed by the request for the particular move or action.

In Liberty Training I, we used primarily a square pen initially and later introduced the horse to a small round pen. The advantage of a round pen over the square pen at this point will be unrestricted flow of movement. We suggest a round pen no larger than 45 feet in diameter. Circus trainers use a 42-foot diameter pen, which is even better for initial schooling. If a horse is flighty, consider using an even smaller pen of 30 to 35 feet, or return to the square pen.

A 60-foot round pen will be ineffective in meaningful Liberty Training, because the horse is out of the handler's immediate sphere of influence and proximity. When using small diameter pens, we school the horses at a walk or a moderate trot and canter for very limited time sessions so as not to tax joints and ligaments. Short sessions help horses keep a fresh mind and good attitude.

A round pen can be used with a well-trained horse or even a troupe of horses and will allow faster paces. When speed is added to even the best rehearsed act, the gaps in each horse's basic training will become evident as their personalities and hierarchical herd positions surface. Do not expect the same level of precision (initially) as was achieved in the smaller rings. The dynamics of each troupe will result in some unique and interesting situations.

Any move that one can do, so can two.

Taba and Holly are linked together and learning to work side by side.

In directing multiple horses, the handler must be capable of magnifying and also diminishing his level of energy to meet the needs of each individual horse. This must be done without transmitting the changes of energy level to the entire troupe. Each horse when called by name should know that you know he knows his name.

Horses learn by watching, known as allelo-mimetic or copycat behavior, so it's a good idea to let horses observe other horses engaged in Liberty Training before being introduced.

Out of the Ordinary and into the Liberty Ring!

Liberty Patterns, also called Sorting Routines, can be simple or complex and include just one horse or an entire troupe. There are lots of logical reasons to add additional horses to the mix! Horses will learn to think and work independently, yet as part of a team they learn to stand their ground or pedestal confidently as other horses work patterns around them. You can easily school and exercise two, three or even up to six or eight horses at one time. Schooling multiple horses will help a handler to develop the ability to keep each individual horse's attention and focus while coaching the entire team.

Although some posturing or horseplay is to be expected at first, it will usually be minimal if the horses are kept moving. Often all that is required to prevent posturing or a horse determined to act up is to point the guider at the horse's nose while taking a step toward him and calling his name. This can be followed either by a verbal reprimand or a calming cue.

If the horses absolutely insist on posturing, add a surcingle and side reins to one or both to help them focus. Before teaching patterns, we introduce the horses to each other initially

Sophie and Miko working in unison at 5 weeks and 8 weeks of age.

by tying them in close but safe proximity to each other and also by ponying them. Some horses naturally get along, while others require a longer period of time to get to know each other.

A troupe of geldings is by nature the easiest grouping to manage. Mixed troupes will give mixed results. In the circus, it is common for all the horses to be stallions. Stallions have a greater degree of crowd-pleasing flash and dash. Additionally circus acts always include a lot of rearing and hind leg walks, and stallions are better equipped physically for these behaviors than laid-back geldings.

We've had mixed acts of mares and geldings that have worked because they were pasture buddies and got along well. Mares and stallions simply do not mix well, except in rare circumstances and with an uncommonly well-behaved stallion.

The inner horse is an adolescent and is linked to an experienced Liberty horse to learn patterns.

Three horses linked together learning patterns. The inside horse is a student. They must be taught to stagger their line-up so Allen can see the inside eye of each horse which helps them focus and be accountable.

The pass through requires that the single horse going the opposite direction is confident and focused.

Take it From the Circus

Circus acts occasionally present mixed exotics such as zebras. Arabians and camels are perhaps the most common mixed act. This requires a LOT of careful introductory preparation. Odd breeds of rare and unusual looking bovines, llamas, even goats and ponies are also presented together. The most unlikely pairing we've ever seen was a rhinoceros and a giraffe presented by the Circus Knie. This was only possible because of the close community of a traveling circus in which the odd animals are housed in close proximity on a daily basis.

A Big and Little Act is always popular and typically will consist of a draft breed or perhaps, a showy Friesian and a pony or miniature horse. Color matching is popular in such acts.

In circus acts the horses always wear a simple surcingle with side reins during training and in performance a fancy patent leather set is used and often decorated with colored ostrich plumes. Bitting minimizes horseplay and posturing between members of the troupe and helps the horse focus on the handler. Occasionally acts are presented featuring the horses with no equipment at all and present the highest standard of the circus arts.

Understanding Cues

In training on the ground, we rely upon a triad of cues, including physical, proximity and verbal, all of which are delivered in a very subtle manner. When training complex moves or behavior chains, the almost invisible cue will help the horse to distinguish which one of many moves he is being asked for. It is habituation, much practice and the horse's nearly perfect memory combined with the handler's skill that will produce a finely finished and polished act.

Same Direction, Single File

After the horse has transitioned from the square pen to working patterns in the round pen, a second horse can be introduced by sending both in the same direction, in single file. A working trot is a good introductory pace although regulating speed will come with practice. Often schooling at the trot is easiest because of the advantage of momentum. When the horse is slowed to a walk he will have time to internalize new behaviors as they can actually think at a slower pace.

The horses can learn gait transitions as a team and even complex patterns. Executing a circle around a pedestal or even figure eights is great for starters. Single file variations include the Waltz, which is a more sophisticated move in which all horses in the line make a full circle or pirouette either one at a time or in unison.

Changing Places is a pattern in which the lead horse follows a cue to turn inward and reverses to take a position at the tail of the line as the other horses continue on in line. This moving rotation is continued so that each horse has a chance to "change" positions.

Each horse is taught to perform patterns separately before they learn to execute them in unison, single file.

If starting with an experienced horse and introducing an inexperienced horse that will not follow, place a neck collar on the lead horse. Attach an extra-long lead rope to the halter of the horse behind him. Quick release snaps are used on both ends of the lead to help avoid an accident.

The lead horse will be acting as an assistant. Care must be taken so neither horse gets a leg over the lead rope.

As a safety precaution create a breakaway connection between the horses. Instead of clipping the lead rope directly to the second horse's halter, use a light piece of string tied in a loop to the halter and clip the lead to the string. This way if there is a problem the string will break before anything serious happens.

Opposite Directions and Altering Herd Hierarchy

Teach two horses to go in opposite directions by attaching a longe line on the inside horse and free longe the outside horse simultaneously. It is natural for them to make faces at each other initially. Initially the inside

horse on the longe line should be kept well out of the way of the oncoming horse. When they are working smoothly side by side, ask the inside horse to reverse. Use a longe whip with a heavy snap to lie out over the back of the outside horse to urge the outside horse to keep moving and to stay in his place.

Horses generally are shy or uncertain when faced with an oncoming horse, especially if the oncoming individual is dominant. It is up to the handler to maintain order and security for the wellbeing and confidence of the shier horse. The exercise of going opposite directions will often increase the confidence of a shy horse when he realizes that the handler is in control or in other words, the herd leader. We've actually seen this exercise change herd dynamics and have a lasting effect of elevating the stature of the shy horse.

Another way to change herd hierarchy for working purposes is to place two horses on separate pedestals a few feet apart. The more dominant horse will predictably "make faces" at the more reticent horse. The handler (you) will step between the pedestals and admonish

The lead horse turns and goes to the back of the line up or "Changes" places until they are once again in the positions they started in.

the dominant horse as you step closer to him. Our friend Sacha Houcke, originally from Circus Knie, says "All bickering has to cease when we enter the (performance) ring."

Horses often make their own decisions about what position they are more comfortable in—rail side or inside while going in opposite directions. We go along with their positioning if it seems to make them comfortable. Add a surcingle and side reins to decrease hesitation to pass the oncoming horse. You might slightly tip the outside horse's head slightly toward the rail and the inside horse's head to the opposite side. When the pattern of behavior is established, the side reins can be eliminated.

Pairing Up Side by Side

If you are like us, we don't have a supply of human assistants so we utilize a trained lead horse that is calm, confident and will follow your directions without hesitation.

We position the lead horse close to the fence at a Halt on the perimeter of the ring and bring the student horse beside him and ask them to stand side-by-side. The vocal cue is "Line Up." The horses can be encouraged to stay abreast by pointing a Guider whip at their noses. The two horses can be clipped together by running a piece of breakable string through the side rings of their halters. For our trained horses, we use 24" lines with a quick release snap on each end.

Speed control and patterns can be perfected while they are clipped together. When the initial pair is working smoothly together, add another pair to the lineup either side by side (four abreast) or in line, nose to tail.

Neck collars are a step up from standard web halters because they allow more comfort and freedom of movement. Also if a horse pulls back there is less chance of torqueing or twisting the horses' heads.

All of the horses making a complete turn at the same time is called the "Waltz."

Pairs of horses can maneuver around pedestals making figures-of-eight and circles just as we do with a single horse. A slower pace is best and should keep horseplay at a minimum.

If the horses start moving faster while side by side, their natural competitiveness will be demonstrated. This is what motivates horses on the racetrack. The challenge is to maintain order and keep them lined up in a way that each horse's inside eye can be seen by the handler. This means they will be slightly staggered and not totally in line abreast. If horses can see the handler, they are more likely to proceed and less likely come out of line.

Two horses make a circle around the horse on the pedestal.

Two sets of horses performing "Musical Pedestals". The pedestal horse must stay in place until the second horse comes up from behind to change places.

Pairing up From Single File

As horses are moving in single file, we point the Guider at the nose of the horse in the lead and ask him to slow his pace as we flick the longe toward the rear feet of the following horse behind to move him forward. We use the vocal cue "Move UP" after calling the horse's name. This takes practice, but the benefits of willing obedience and self-control are well worth the time invested.

Separate Tasks

Call out the most reliable horse and ask him to "Step Up" on a pedestal as the other (or several) continues along the perimeter of the pen. When the "parked" horse is reliable in staying on his place, the second horse can circle the pedestal as part of a pattern. Variations can include one horse parked on a pedestal as another sits on a Bean Bag or retrieves an object or ball. The variations are virtually endless.

Change and the Double Waltzing

With multiple horses the achievable variations in a routine are only limited by your imagination. A simple change in which the lead horse changes places (to tail position) can be varied so that the second horse begins to change (or turn) simultaneously as they are nose to tail. The tight circling becomes a Double Waltz, which is a beautiful maneuver generally seen only in the traditional circus. Horses marching as pairs can also Double Waltz which is four horses waltzing as two pairs.

Tips

- Pay attention to the spacing and teach each horse to rate his speed when working in single file. They can be taught to "Spread out" or "Move up" when called by name.

- When schooling two (or more) horses abreast, teach the inside horses to stay slightly behind the outer horse(s) so the handler can see the inside eye of each horse in the line. If the horse can see the handler, it is easier for him to focus, understand and respond to the requests and cues he is given.

- It is normal herd behavior for horses to try to "hide" behind another horse. If this happens, gently urge the "hiding" horse to continue forward movement with the snap of a whip behind him, or have an assistant on the outside of the ring to keep him moving. Try to anticipate if the horse is going to stop and hide and prevent it before it actually happens.

- We strongly suggest using professional grade training whips and Guider whips in Liberty Training. Substituting livestock sticks and plastic longe whips will not give the accuracy and control needed for this work.

Make it a Circus!

Virtually any pattern that can be ridden in an enclosed area can be duplicated with one horse or multiple horses at liberty. Pick your favorite and add a few more horses, you can be your own drill team or even your own circus!

Remember—you don't have to run away to join the circus—with a willing horse or two, and a little imagination, you can have one in your own backyard.

Further instructions are included in the DVD *"Liberty Training II"*

Case Studies: Using the Tricks in Real Life

The Trick Horse Companion

Trick for Standing Ground in a crisis

It was dusk on the last day of a riding trip to Montana when we were surprised by the sound of thundering hooves as a herd of mules bolted out of the trees, onto the trail, running straight toward us. They were being herded with a four wheeler by an outfitter that didn't expect other riders on the trail. My horse whirled to run (yes, he dumped me) but ran straight to my friend's mare, Elle and hid behind her. Kristi quickly caught up my horse's reins, faced the oncoming stampede and told Elle to "stand" her ground. She had learned to stand confidently in her liberty training which included having as many as 6 other horses work patterns with her and around her.

Working two (or more) horses together while at liberty in a round pen is a simple way of changing herd dynamics and creating boldness and bravery in a group situation.

The physical act of facing head on and closely passing a horse coming in the opposite direction can give a horse confidence to stand his ground in almost any circumstance. A horse learns in just a revolution or two in the round pen that you control the other horses and he is safe with you as the herd leader.

Working together promotes harmony and trust among the troupe members of all ages.

Targeting Trick for a steady mount

Standing quietly and safely for mounting is a must for all trail horses and face it, as we age we need a horse to stand absolutely still in any terrain and hold the position for up to a minute or more for mounting. There is often no margin for error.

One trick to assure a solid mounting stance is to teach a side pass to a target such as a mounting block or large rock, even to a person. A side pass to a person is always followed by a park out as a distinguishable end point. On a steep or narrow trail, we use only the park out position as we would not have room for a side pass. We seldom mount from the park position because it puts additional stress on the horse's joints yet it IS nice to be able to when you really need it.

Whether on a mountainside or next to a pedestal at home, Elle stood stock still for mounting.

The Trick Horse Companion

Tricks for Step Ups and Bridges

In Yellowstone Park we encountered a lot of interesting and yes, rather intimidating bridges. I must admit the long, swaying suspension bridge made my adrenaline rise. Our horses balked initially but the familiar "step up" cue gave them courage to step up with the front feet and stand still. This was followed by a couple seconds of reassurance before we continued on across. It was interesting that once our horses heard the hollow sound of their front feet landing on the wooden bridge- a similar sound as on a pedestal, they became confident.

One of the goals of pedestal training is to create in the horse a conditioned and obedient response to the "Step Up" cue. When the response is habituated in a controlled training setting it can be practiced on the trail with large rocks, stumps, other obstacles and bridges.

Sabre learned in her first week of life to sit on the bean bag and to lie down with Allen's help.

The Trick Horse Companion

Sabre Takes Laying Down Seriously

When Sabre was three months old, her dam Sharrifah had to be taken to Texas A&M University large animal hospital for an examination. Sabre soon grew tired of standing in hand and not being allowed to nurse.

We asked the assistants to bring in some large lay down mats as are used in equine surgery. They did and we asked Sabre to "Sit Down" on them while a number of veterinary interns had their pictures taken beside a sitting horse. They were all very interested in her ability and obedience.

As more time passed and she grew restless because she wanted to nurse, we asked her to Lie Down. She obediently did so and happily snoozed during her mother's entire two-hour procedure. As we were leaving the hospital that day with Sharrifah and Sabre, there was another foal being literally dragged into the hospital by four vet assistants. The foal was not larger than Sabre but was virtually uncontrollable because it obviously had not been to school yet. The assistants told us this was the normal way foals acted when they were brought in. We were sure happy Sabre had started school early! There is a better way.

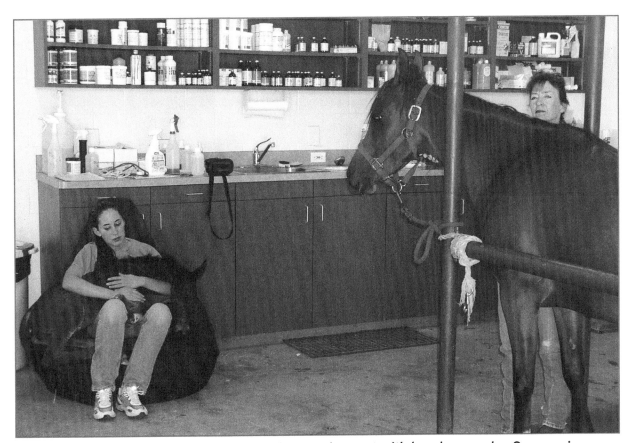

Sabre was content to sleep through the entire appointment with her dam nearby. Once again, a familiar object and position gave her confidence in an unfamiliar circumstance.

Shallanna's Trust
Sets Her Free

Shallana is Donna Moore's Arabian mare. Sue and Donna taught her many tricks, including to Lie Down on cue. One day as Donna was unloading Shallana from a trailer in the stable yard, the mare slipped while backing out. She slid down a grassy slope and flipped over into a wire fence. Her feet were hung up in the fence and if she had fought to free herself, the consequences could have been dire. Donna soothed her and told her to "Lie Down" and stay where she was, upside down!

The mare's trust and obedience and Donna's reassuring calmness gave her the courage to stay still until her feet could be untangled. Donna then gave her the cue to get up, and she was essentially unharmed and calm.

Shallanna

This three week old filly's early pedestal training gave her confidence to cross the teeter totter even on her first try.

Adding the pedestal at the end of the ramp made the situation seem familiar for these miniatures even though they had never seen the trailer before.

Trailer Loading Made Easy

Miko and Sophie were miniature foals born at our ranch and raised in Enhanced Foal Training. In preparation for the move to their owners' ranches, we taught them to load in a trailer. Their dams although raised domestically had always been herded into a trailer with no real education applied to the situation.

Miko and Sophie were both accomplished in pedestal work before their trailer loading education was started. We set the foal pedestal at the ramp of the trailer and let the foals with dams beside them explore the situation. In less than five minutes the fillies could be sent to the pedestal from a distance and then into the trailer. This gave their dams confidence to load up as well. Trailer training can be a normal part of a horse's life and not something to be feared by either horse or human.

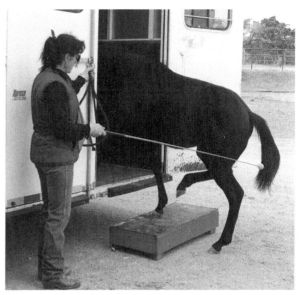

Familiar objects such as the pedestal give a horse of any age confidence to "Step Up" into the trailer and to back and "Step Down."

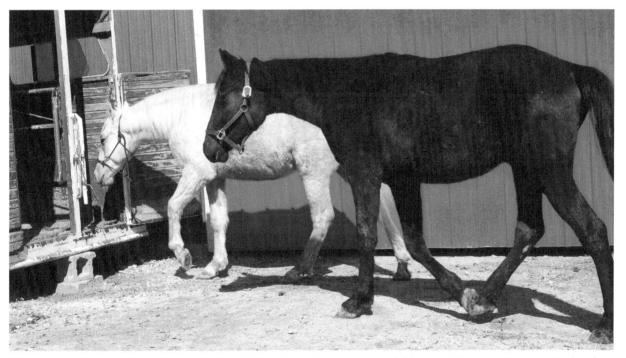

These yearlings combined pedestal and liberty training and could be sent from a distance to load up side by side.

Epilogue

We encourage each of you to engage with your horse in a way that allows him to understand you are his friend, by giving him a working language in pantomime and then "hearing" him with your mind, heart and soul. What he will give back will be more than you ever expected.

Where you start can be determined by your goals and your horse's needs and innate talents. We know the amount of information we have shared can be overwhelming; however, committing even half an hour a day will be a good beginning.

In this book, we've shared how our horses respond and bond through Enlightened Trick Horse Training, and we are committed to helping you elevate your horse's relationship with you to the same level. We have been greatly blessed to make this our life's work. We welcome your calls, and emails and visits. We are here to offer you the support required.

Enhanced Trick Horse Training has proven beneficial and even lifesaving in many real-life situations, some of which we have shared in the preceding pages.

–Allen & Sue

Additional Information,

updates, books, videos and other online learning may be found at:

http://www.ImagineaHorse.com

Online Forum

You may enjoy our Yahoo Discussion Group titled "Imagine a Horse". The group has thousands of members all around the globe that mentor each other on trick horse training. This is what we call good, clean fun! Allen has been actively engaged with the group members for many years, and many have visited us and attended trick horse camp. http://groups.yahoo.com/group/Imaginea-Horse/

If you would like to be included in our exciting and informational electronic newsletter, just click on the link on our web site.

Buy:

http://www.ImagineaHorse.com

Bean Bags
Hobbles
Horse-Friendly Training Whips
Nip Buster
Training Treats
Surcingles and Belly Bands
Horse Tuff Big Balls
Toss and Retrieve Balls
Frisbees (with modified tab)

How to Make

Pedestal - See Appendix

Suggested Reading & Resources

A Pictorial History of Performing Horses, by Charles Philip Fox

Adam's Task: Calling Animals by Name, by Vicki Hearne

Breaking and Riding, by James Fillis

Classical Circus Equitation, by H.J. Lijsen and Sylvia Stainer

Creative Horsemanship, by Charles De Kunffy

Don't Shoot the Dog, by Karen Pryor

Horse Sense, by Henry Blake

How to Train A _____: From aardvarks to zebras, applied behavior science has a rational prescription for creating behavior change, by Patricia Barlow-Irick, PhD

How to Train Your Horse: a Complete Guide to Making an Honest Horse, by Anthony Amaral

llustrated Horse Training, by Horace Hayes

My Dancing White Horses, by Alois Podhajsky

My Horses My Teachers, by Alois Podhajsky

Natural Horsemanship Explained by Dr. Robert M. Miller D.V.M.

Training the Haute E'cole or High School Horse, by Chuck Grant

Talking With Horses, by Henry Blake

The Body Language of Horses, by Bonnie Ledbetter

The Classic Encyclopedia of Horses, by Dennis Magner

The Development of Modern Riding, by Vladimir Littauer

The Fascinating Techniques of Training Movie Horses, by Anthony Amaral

The Revolution in Horsemanship and What it Means to Mankind by Dr. Robert M. Miller D.V.M.

The Ultimate Horse Behavior and Training Book, by Linda Tellington-Jones and Bobbie Lieberman

There Are No Problem Horses, Only Problem Riders, by Mary Twelveponies

Thinking With Horses by Hnery Blake

Understanding Ancient Secrets of the Horse's Mind by Dr. Robert M. Miller D.V.M.

Appendix A
Basic Pedestal Construction

The Trick Horse Companion

Imagine A Horse
Master Trick Trainers

HORSE PEDESTAL CONSTRUCTION INSTRUCTIONS

APPROXIMATE SIZE: 23" x 47" x 15" HIGH

NOTE: THE DIMENSIONS MAY BE ADJUSTED TO CREATE A PEDESTAL OF ANY SIZE.

IMAGINE A HORSE©
WWW.IMAGINEAHORSE.COM
512-264-0442

HORSE PEDESTAL CONSTRUCTION INSTRUCTIONS

MATERIALS LIST:

(1) SHEET 3/4" BC OR AC EXTERIOR GRADE PLYWOOD
(1) 4" x 4" X 6 FT TREATED WOOD POST
(1) 2" x 4" x 6 ft TREATED WOOD STUD
(25) 2-1/2" DECKING SCREWS
(70) 1-3/4" #8 DECKING SCREWS
(25) ROOFING NAILS
(1) 24" x 48" STALL MAT
CARPENTER'S GLUE
OIL-BASED PRIMER PAINT
OIL-BASED ENAMEL PAINT

RECOMMENDED TOOLS:

TABLE SAW
ROUTER
HAND SANDER
BELT SANDER
SCREW GUN
FINISH NAILER OR HAMMER
MEASURING TAPE
PENCIL

PG-2

HORSE PEDESTAL CONSTRUCTION INSTRUCTIONS

STEP ONE:

- TAKE TWO CUTS 12" WIDE THE LENGTH OF THE PLYWOOD SHEET. THESE TWO PIECES WILL BE THE LONG SIDES AND END PIECES. (PIECE A)

- CUT THE OTHER HALF OF THE PLYWOOD SHEET IN HALF. THESE TWO PIECES WILL BE USED FOR THE DOUBLE THICKNESS TOP. (PIECE B)

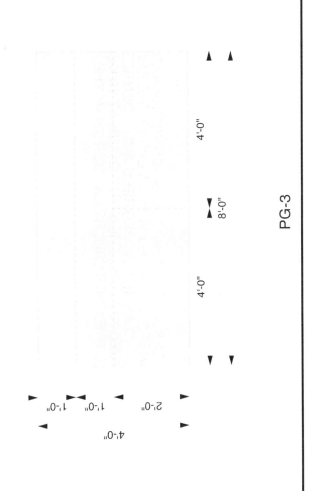

PG-3

HORSE PEDESTAL CONSTRUCTION INSTRUCTIONS

STEP TWO:

- THE END AND SIDE PIECES ARE CUT SO THE SIDES TIP INWARD AT A 15 DEGREE ANGLE FROM THE GROUND. WHERE THE SIDES WILL OVERLAP THE ENDS, HE ENDS WILL NEED TO BE CUT AT A COMPOUND ANGLE, 15 DEGREES AND 5 DEGREES. ON A TABLE SAW, TILT THE BLADE 5 DEGREES AND SET THE SLIDE GUIDE AT 15 DEGREES. REMEMBER THE INSIDE FACE OF ALL THE ENDS WILL BE LARGER THAN THE OUTSIDE FACES BY THE FACTOR OF 5 DEGREES.

Blade tilt 5 degrees

75 degrees

Slide guide

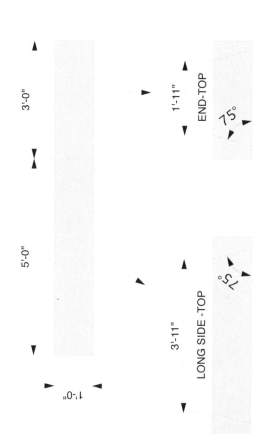

5'-0"

3'-0"

1'-0"

3'-11"

1'-11"

LONG SIDE -TOP

75°

END-TOP

75°

PG-4

HORSE PEDESTAL CONSTRUCTION INSTRUCTIONS

STEP THREE:

- ASSEMBLE THE SIDES TO THE ENDS WITH 3d NAILS. DO NOT SCREW INTO THE EDGES OF THE PLYWOOD.

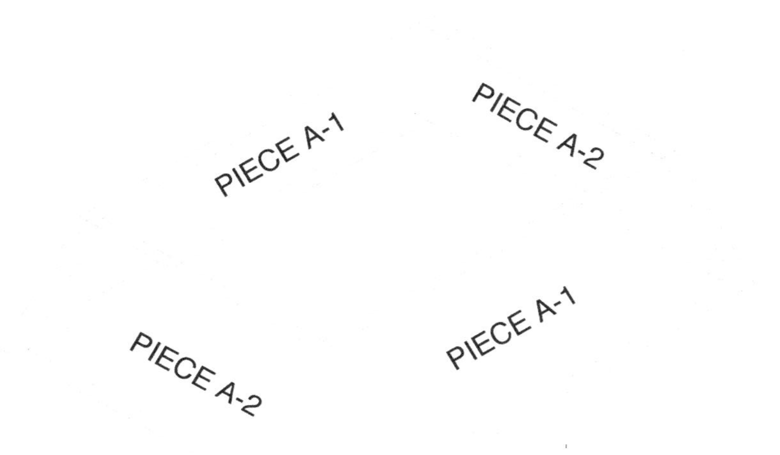

PIECE A-2

PIECE A-1

PIECE A-1

PIECE A-2

PG-5

HORSE PEDESTAL CONSTRUCTION INSTRUCTIONS

STEP FOUR:

- CUT THE 2' X 4' PIECE TO MAKE THE FALSE TOP. THE FALSE TOP IS A PIECE OF PLYWOOD THAT IS HIDDEN FROM VIEW ON THE FINISHED PEDESTAL AND ADDS A SECOND LAYER TO THE TOP. CUT A 15 DEGREE BEVEL ON ALL FOUR EDGES SO THAT IT WILL FIT SNUG INSIDE THE PEDESTAL ASSEMBLY.

- INSERT THE FALSE TOP FROM THE BOTTOM. USE PLENTY OF GLUE AT THE JOINT. THIS WILL KEEP MOISTURE FROM ACCUMULATING IN THE JOINT, WHICH WOULD MAKE THE ENDS OF THE PLYWOOD SWELL. THE TIGHTER THE TOLERANCE RESULTS IN A BETTER AND STRONGER GLUE JOINT.

- TACK THE FALSE TOP IN PLACE FROM THE BOTTOM SIDE WITH 3d FINISHING NAILS OR A FINISH NAILER.

BEVEL ALL EDGES

PIECE B

CUT TO FIT

PG-6

False top inserted from bottom

HORSE PEDESTAL CONSTRUCTION INSTRUCTIONS

STEP FIVE:

- GLUE BLOCKS WILL GO ALL AROUND THE INSIDE WHERE THE SIDES MEET THE BOTTOM OF THE FALSE TOP. TO MAKE THE BLOCKS, RIP A 2X4 LENGTHWISE WITH A 15 DEGREE CUT YIELDING TWO LONG GLUE BLOCKS. CUT TO MAKE TWO PIECES APPROXIMATELY 46" AND TWO PIECES APPROXIMATELY 22" LONG. MEASURE ONCE MORE, THEN CUT TO FIT AND TACK THEM IN PLACE.

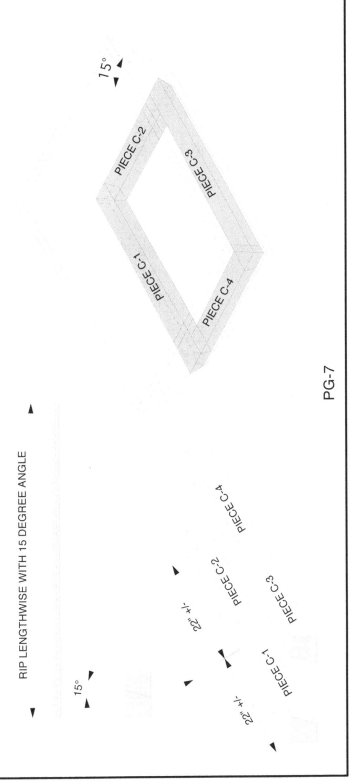

RIP LENGTHWISE WITH 15 DEGREE ANGLE

15°

22" +/-

22" +/-

PIECE C-1

PIECE C-2

PIECE C-3

PIECE C-4

15°

PIECE C-1

PIECE C-2

PIECE C-3

PIECE C-4

PG-7

205

HORSE PEDESTAL CONSTRUCTION INSTRUCTIONS

STEP SIX:

- CUT A TREATED 4X4 INTO FOUR PIECES MEASURING ABOUT 17" LONG. REDUCE THE 4X4 PIECES TO A 3X3 BY CUTTING AWAY THE MOST UNDESIRABLE SIDES AND MAKE A 5 DEGREE CUT TO THE LENGTH OF ONE SIDE, ALLOWING THE LEG TO FIT SNUG INTO THE CORNER. CUT THE ENDS OF EACH BY SETTING THE TABLE SAW BLADE 15 DEGREES AND THE SLIDE GUIDE AT 75 DEGREES TO MAKE A COMPOUND CUT, ALLOWING THE LEG TO FIT SNUG AGAINST THE BOTTOM OF THE GLUE BLOCKS.

17" +/-

PIECE D-1   PIECE D-2   PIECE D-3   PIECE D-4

Blade tilt
5 degrees

Leg end cuts

Slide Guide
75 degrees

Blade tilt
15 degrees

PG-8

HORSE PEDESTAL CONSTRUCTION INSTRUCTIONS

STEP SEVEN:

- USE A 3" SCRAP AS A MEASURING GUIDE AND DRAW A LINE AROUND THE EXPOSED LEG USING THE BOTTOM EDGE OF THE SIDES FOR SUPPORT. THIS WILL GIVE A 3" LEG THAT IS CUT PARALLEL TO THE GROUND. ONCE THE LEGS ARE FITTED INTO THE CORNERS, SECURE THEM BY USING PLENTY OF "TITE-BOND II" GLUE (A SEMI-WATERPROOF EXTERIOR GRADE CARPENTER'S GLUE). SECURE THE LEGS WITH 5 TO 6 1-3/4" #8 DECKING OR COARSE THREAD SHEETROCK SCREWS ON BOTH FACES OF PLYWOOD (SIDES AND ENDS, MEANING 10 TO 12 SCREWS PER LEG). USE A 1/2" ROUND-OVER BIT IN A ROUTER TO ROUND EXPOSED EDGES OF THE LEG.

USE 3" SCRAP

PG-9

207

HORSE PEDESTAL CONSTRUCTION INSTRUCTIONS

STEP EIGHT:

- TURN THE PEDESTAL OVER AND MEASURE FOR THE EXPOSED TOP PIECE OF PLYWOOD. CUT TOP TO FIT AND USE PLENTY OF GLUE TO LAMINATE IT TO THE FALSE TOP. SCREW THE TOP DOWN USING 2-1/2" #8 SCREWS ABOUT EVERY 6 INCHES. POSITION THE SCREWS SO THAT THEY GO INTO THE GLUE BLOCKS ON THE UNDERSIDE. SCREW THE SIDES AND ENDS TO THE NOW SECURE GLUE BLOCKS (DO NOT SCREW INTO THE SIDES OF PLYWOOD). DRILLING A COUNTER SINK SCREW HOLE FOR EACH SCREW POSITION WILL YIELD A BETTER LOOKING FINISHED PRODUCT.

- USE A BELT SANDER WITH A 36 GRIT BELT TO ROUGH SAND ALL EDGES. USE AN 80 GRIT BELT TO FINISH. USE AN 80 OR 100 GRIT IN A HAND SANDER TO MAKE A PAINT GRADE SMOOTH FINISH. ROUND ALL CORNERS WITH AT LEAST A 1/2" ROUTER BIT.

TOP PLYWOOD PIECE

PG-10

HORSE PEDESTAL CONSTRUCTION INSTRUCTIONS

STEP NINE:

- FILL ALL CRACKS AND SCREW HOLES WITH BONDO (AN AUTOMOTIVE BODY PUTTY) OR SOLVENT-BASED WOOD FILLER (SUCH AS FARMWOOD BRAND). LATEX BASED FILLERS WILL NOT HOLD UP IN EXTERIOR CONDITIONS.

- PAINT TWO COATS OF OIL-BASED PRIMER. SAND BETWEEN COATS. THEN APPLY A MINIMUM OF TWO COATS OF OIL-BASED ENAMEL. THIS WILL TAKE LONGER TO DRY, BUT PROVIDES A NICE FINISH THAT MAY BE RECOATED AS NEEDED.

- CUT TO FIT A 1/2" RUBBER STALL MAT TO FIT THE TOP. NAIL DOWN WITH ROOFING NAILS.

STALL MAT TOP

PG-11

Appendix B
Inspirational Photos

Sheryl Crow was carried to the stage for her concert by Lady C. She wowed the audience with this Rear as Sue cued her. (Photo: courtesy of the Houston Livestock Show and Rodeo.)

The Trick Horse Companion

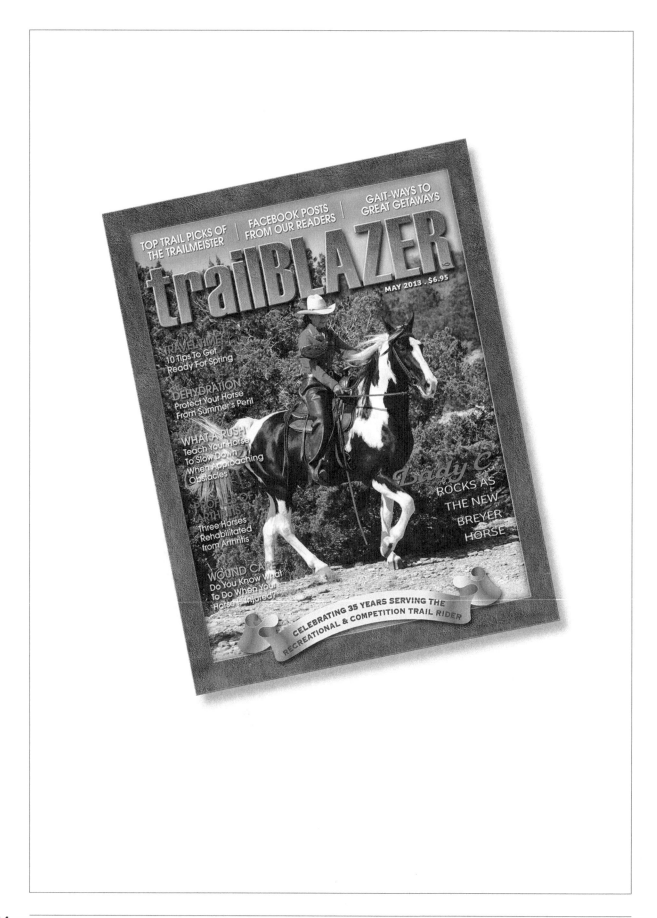

OCT/NOV 2004

Arabian Horse
Official Publication of the Arabian Horse Association

MAGAZINE

NEW—*REGISTRATION SPECIAL*
See page 146

Presidential Forum
AHA Candidates Debate the Issues

2004 Youth Nationals
Show Sets New Records

Spooking Solutions
Create a Confident Horse

The Trick Horse Companion

The Trick Horse Companion

The Trick Horse Companion

www.imagineahorse.com

CPSIA information can be obtained at www.ICGtesting.com
Printed in the USA
LVOW01*0056021014

406901LV00001B/1/P